The Unspoken, a book of poetry by Bob Holman. is proof that difficult can be brought together with illuminating. Bob Holman is rolling all his runes and Q-Lists (question lists) together in this book. He has fully harvested his "po-mind," or Bard Brain.

These poems reveal how good willed and open he is. The plethora of epithalamia, "praise poems," and salutes to friends stand out. And especially poems to his wife Elizabeth Murray and their children.

He is seethingly on a vast search. And in this search he's absolutely unafraid to flash his quick-flowing torrents of words, lighting up the pages like millionfold assertions fast-mentioned in a fast-packed life-talk.

These poems can be seen as those of a transrealist chant-man, so committed to good issues, you wonder how he keeps his shoulder, sometimes so ouchingly, to the Wheel. He is Always on the Move, his clipboard bulging with variegated projects, and always annotating and jotting verse on this surface, that, and the Other. You become amazed how he ponders things on such a huge and multi-evented canvas. Such as the love and zeal he commits for the protection and enhancement of endangered languages around the world.

Bob Holman solidified his reputation on the stage of Perf-Po, or performance poetry. For 8 years in the '80s and '90s Bob was the co-director of the Nuyorican Poets Cafe. In a vital exploration of the lovemaking between performance and poetry, Holman founded and hosted Nuyorican's far-famed series of Poetry Slams. He has also been active in the theater, as a producer and author. And he's produced a number of documentaries.

Of course Bob Holman, in these years which threaten a wasting nuclear war, is very aware that the poetry has to exist in raw lines of writing on printed surfaces, to lurk on fluttering pages on post-apocalyptic beaches. That's where we encounter his book, *The Unspoken.*

Read it and ponder, then go into action. **—Ed Sanders**

What a lion Bob is, in search of and in defense of languages… and rock'n'roller. These poems are smart, funny and fulla fire, perfect friends with all the ears of earth's bards. Built to float, borne over waters, sailing with song, traveling with tongues.

—Tom Pickard

Bob Holman is a one-of-a-kind poet/musician/playwright/engineer of language, and THE UNSPOKEN is a master work. **—Dael Orlandersmith**

Bob Holman is widely known as the consummate spoken word maestro. Now he applies his explosive talents to the dark matter of the unspoken word. He helps us to see what can't be heard -- "So very carefully uns⸺ ⸺ing the turtle shell to reveal the sleeping mouse." **—Elaine Equi**

Bob Holman is an Action Figure of Speech.   *—Raymond Nat Turner*

The widely-traveled wisdom collector and poetry catalyst Bob Holman has an encyclopedist's view of shining light on the many terra incognitas of the human condition, as well as of his own psyche. His new books continue to make compelling music and teach enthusiasm and courage. Holman is open like Apollinaire's "upside-down heart." The river of his poetry has widened considerably in the many years he has promoted, researched and written his song. His new books are free, wise, and drenched in the light of decades of service to our art. Bob Holman is the President of Poetry.

—Andrei Codrescu

Bob Holman is poetry in the flesh. He has not only blazed a trail, he has lived the trail. In a poetic landscape of YouTube views and social media likes, Bob's work is now more important and authentic to the soul of the movement he helped build than ever before.

—Cary Goldberg

Poetry is the insanity that makes us sane. Bob Holman is a true poet. Why not be in love? What is the big goddam reason for not being in love? It's raining poems, and we are the grass they nourish. He swims in the Sargasso Sea of the double-alphabet – and we swim with him. Bob Holman is the Rumi of the Bowery.   *—Sparrow*

Like his idol Frank O'Hara and former teacher/mentor Kenneth Koch, Bob Holman's poems in *The (Un)Spoken* draw on a boundless love for the act/art of collaboration. They move seamlessly between the praise form & elegy, the ode & occasional poem, & the result is a multitudinous libretto of poems retrieved over two decades, made with/&in tribute to the poet's late wife, & his global community of fellow bards, choreographers, cinematographers, educators, elders, musicians, & painters. "Hellbent in Twisting the Sky/Setting Fire to Ocean/Lightning Strikes Under Water," Holman's poems also signal a deeper humanism in his speaker/s, "finally leaping through the window of faith" as they urge the reader/listener to "roar each moment into being/ knowing it's each other we're freeing." This irresistible new yawp makes plain that "[d]eath don't stop here/a tree that blossoms one by one," compelled by the poet's Septuagenarian double beginner spirit for whom "Language is what the stones thought of/when they wanted to dance."   *—Paolo Javier*

In *The Unspoken*, Holman channels all the channels – kids on the street, famous poets, hipsters, musicians, painters. In fact, all poetries, from the Fox Trot to Ezra Pound, get a shout-out, nowhere more profoundly than in the generous selection of Praise Poems. Dig in, and Smooth Sailing! All Praise Holman!   *—Vincent Katz*

~~Bob Holman and~~

The ^Un^Spoken

~~Word Movement~~

OPEN UP!
Hope-epe
hopen-u
pen-up
open up!!

as non-oralized by
BOB HOLMAN

YBK Publishers   NEW YORK
BOWERY BOOKS   No. 13

Dedicated to Your Birthday!
and to Steve Cannon and Stuart Hanlon

Friendship is Underrated

The Unspoken

Copyright © 2019 by Bob Holman

YBK Publishers, Inc.   Bowery Books
39 Crosby Street   308 Bowery
New York, NY 10013   New York, NY
www.ybkpublishers.com   www. bowerypoetry.com

ISBN:978-1-936411-57-3

Library of Congress Catalog Card Number 2019948601

Cover drawing by Paul Zinkievich. Image and poem originally published as a Hard Press postcard by Jeffrey Cyphers Wright.

Cover design by Mike Tully

Manufactured in the United States of America for distribution in
North and South America or in the United Kingdom or Australia
when distributed elsewhere.

For more information, visit www.ybkpublishers.com

OPEN UP!

Hope-ope-
hopen-up
pen-up

open up!!

Poems

Movements

Praise!

This Is It!

Notes

Prelude

Hey You!

While I was writing Hey you
I was saying "Hey you!" to you

By the Book

Whenever someone reminds me
To do something "by the book"
I always ask them if they can lend me some cash
So I can go ahead and buy the book

By the Book

Before you can do something "by the book"
You have to write the damn book

Performance Poem

Voices. Voices. Listen, my heart,
as only saints have listened;
until the gigantic call lifted them off the ground;
yet they kept on, impossibly, kneeling
and didn't notice at all:
so complete was their listening.
—Rilke, The First Elegy

He's diving off the front of the stage!
You better bring the house lights up some,
The audience can't see him.

1

He's still screaming,
Screaming and dancing
And he's twirling the mic—
I dunno, should we turn off the mic?
I dunno, turn it up?
He's running around, he's twirling and
He's still like reading.
The book is in his hands, sort of, the people
Seem to like it, they're into it—
Maybe it's part of the act.

Well, if it's part of the act he shoulda told us!
Now he's in the back of the house—he's
Still going strong. This is pretty
Amazing. I've never seen anything
Like this! He's running out
Of the theater—I can hear him screaming
In the lobby. He's back in the house!
What's he saying?—It's something about,
It sounds like *"Lake Snore Freedom"*....
I dunno. *"Break Down Reason"*?
Oh shit! Oh shit oh shit—he's got a gun!

Christ! wait—awww, it's just one of those pop guns.
Shoots like firecrackers or popcorn or—
What about the hat? Still wearing the hat.
Holy—he's dying now, I mean he's acting like that,
Like he's dying. This is it for poetry in this house man,
I've had it.

He's just lying there.
The audience is wailing, they're *keening*
You know, like at a wake. No, I don't think
He's really dead. He's getting back up, see, I told
You—it's all part of the act!

It's all part of the end of the world.

What am I, the guy's father?

Come here! Look at the monitor yourself.

He's ditched the mic somewhere,

Should I go get the mic?

Look! oh my God—he's, what's it called,

He's going up, he's *levitating*!

Holy shit! The roof, the roof is going up

Music is coming in

The crowd's up outta their chairs, man this is it

This is it I'm telling you—

Raising the fucking roof is what he's doing!

Now he's back on the stage with his poetry stuff

He never left the stage

It's what his poem was about

I'm just saying what he's saying

Through the headset

Yeah, he's good

He's pretty good alright

But I could write something like that

Anybody could write something like that

The Death of Poetry

You were invited there

You overslept again

What's your excuse this time

You missed the boat/vote/rote/moat/bloat/goat. . . . You missed the goat

The book was printed up

The words all ran together

The pages black with ink

So the faux po's used invisible stink

A fluke inside the coffin as they swing it
Up on their shoulders
En route to gravesite
Finally inside *in* Grave ride riptide

Woho, The Death of Poetry!
Mercifully fast
Only lasted a millennium or two
Art of the Past

No mo po
Get down to bidness
Po's no show
Good riddance

The view was dark/hark/lark/bark/stark...The view was stark
The time was passing slo/emotion
The day was calm and a-foggy, cool and a-balmy,
April is the cruelest . . . coolest! . . . .

The creeps were creeping out
Launching eulogy missiles at the street
The words' worth opposite beat
The drummer's melodizing feet

Typewriters on parade
Walt'n'Emily rolling grave
Nothing left save to save
The Death of Poetry
Computer thing
Neuter thing
Belligerent knucklehead
Brat art teeth shred

Flesh word battery nozzle
Blue skinny grenade carousal
Itchy mean grouse rasp kiss
Whatta life death is
The Death of Poetry

Vast and Various and Unspoken

Better'n Posterity! A little Wow Now!
You see what you don't say, see,

Or, say what you don't see. Say,
There are "languages in air" (trees)
You do not see them (you are insects) and
Then you cannot speak the language anyway

So you are stuck forever inside your head
Seeing most amazing Thing of Danger to Change
The Whole World and so you go: *Mffla
Prakalakashakatakalulu,* and
You are not even Finnish yet!

But see ing as how ev er y th ing
Changes into oth er thi ngs you
Have stirred up bees' hornets' helmets

And people are looking wisely, or as wisely
As praying manti can look at you

The stick the walking stick the sheleighley
Not even knowing how to spell shillelagh

Door stopper is (or, becomes) dictionary

Dictionary becomes (or, is) (you were born with dictionary as)
Your favorite word because it is all words
Nah that would be Alphabet Universe. Or You.

God breathes slowly. Here comes the Unspoken Word.

God is a solitary salsero in the Bronx, all the poems
Are in the fireplace—kindling. The Book
Of Book props window open. But Fire
Escape is broken so Fire does/does not escape

So they open the refrigerator and there you are
Still waiting for them to understand the crucial
Mffla Prakalakashakatakalulu. Luckily (Luckily?), you
Forgot to die frozen so perfectly blued life-like. But luckily
(Luckily!) Madame Tussaud is right there to bid on
Your cryogenically-preserved salsero voice
Singing about the "peck peck" of pigeons
As if all we did was pecking

We all all day just peck peck
Like pigeons do do
Everybody wants
Comforts of the middle class
Nobody can pay for them
Another deep political philosophical conundrum
Famous Model wearing Kleenex bikini speaking
Through Gertrude Stein's brain

Voice in bikini
Stuck on prairie, desert
Stuck in ocean, river
Stuck on subway, the Token Rider and Her Staff of Mighty Beings
I wouldn't be so sure about that, Sir
The Captain of the Committee to Create Committees
To Form the Institution clenches dagger twixt his mustache hairs

And plunges like a safe
Out the seductive window
Ahoy! Speak, you Motherfucker!
Mffla Prakalakashakatakalulu!

The Unspoken Word

Hello?

　　Hello?

There is no talking! This is dumb piece
　　　　　　　of paper covered with blotto stains
　　　　grease lips all over it.
Can the can't.

　　　　Eat the words.

The core is language.
　　Eat that, too!

Once upon a tiny little once.
But often, more than likely. What happens is this:
The truth is in the telling, the tasting.
Add salt.
Corrode the pipeline.

　　　　　　Art and Industry swagger down the aisle, hand in claw.

I have been asked to speak to you
　　　　but my tongue
　　has another opinion.

Right is wrong.

Whenever her fingers slide into the machine, Africa winces with pain.

Terror and treachery make fine breakfast.

As I was saying towards end of line, prose.

Taste a fat chunk o' prose. Is all prose, baked, wilted? Except rose.

Freedom is pregnant with democracy's bastard, all lies.

The poor cannot get to sleep.

Steady goes the junk food.

Merciless climate,

The homeless congregate for more than warmth.

Slow reptilian devolution. Music is bought and silence is the price. Meanwhile, there is no meanwhile. This is not the end. This is.

PS

Will respond more fully when moon rises and I can read the book
To sleep.

Waiting for Never (The Unspoken Word)

I propose this chilly morning to the world
Itself awaiting a duh flash spilt tongue lift
From and over the cloud suture and astral
Bludgeon with pigeon slowly
Dusting powdery snow of never

Quite spring the Bowery and people walking
Past the door they are invited into
Calm betrayal of blue caution how
To challenge everyday stupidity of knock?
Go in, my dear Friend, how friendship
Covers the moment grave gravy I crave
Potential even as the salty rock diamond
Stalactite drips efficiency into the troll's mug
Bard soap and melt the hair
Retrieve all hope that rocks out the tear
And then they would respond, all
One of them via ventricle the cerebral-spinal
Ocean speaks to the shore and the river craves
The rafter to the soldier and her kin a reminder
Of uniform plaid crazed blue stain barbering
The remainder with keener resplendence
As the tough sloughs and the leaner surrenders
All over the floor dancing swans and minstrels
Affiliate of the sore spore's delight to restore
Capturing the glance moment's pleasure in
Significant disarray for never and a day off
Just to wish a happening birthday man the relish
Of forgetfulness and the king of dome under sun
Meshing alluvial restraint to the mitred velocity
Hand appears to float around like a magic trick
Without the magician and church sprouts
Up like cornstalk silk and one wink fractures
Morningside domain's dominion of predominant
Dominoes and prevailing veils waiting pun
To vanish the child into the man the woman
The ages suit up and rashly billow a fragrance
All too balmy and proficient

The Super Image

Obliterating the subtle text a blot of ink from Godsquid
Bottom of page a footnote pounds brute beat
Meaning willow with small stone that reads
"Here Lies Lies"

The Soul is convinced there's no such thing as soul

The turtles need convincing
They keep wandering offffff
With very important jails

At the bottom of the page a lame flamenco's jump-up
Even though nobody comes
Everybody's seen it
Even though the subtitles are retranslated
On a daily basis by a poet who actually has a paying job
Making these new poems so trenchant running
Across the bottom of the screen
Atop the opera conducted by electric rain

Silence

Put hat over yawn
Make it dawn

Taos

Winds born here
Softer touch than vision
The unspoken

Snake

All of it and all the time, Snake, you and your shedding. Try shedding your heart like you do your skins. Understand the new color spectrum, sung to the strum of the bees. The Unspoken Word.

And that's what I'm waiting for, way back in the back of the bus, deep in the cavern of the bus, the place you didn't even know was here, darkest blackest screamingest soundlessest soullessest place you call Unspoken, that's where I am, that's where I'm coiled and waiting, under that stinking seat, down under where the axles grind the road to bits, down where there's dirt to pay, where the poem is prayer and you never learn to pray.

Letter to Elizabeth

The days go by like wild horses. How are you?

I just broke through the chakra membrane and called your phone thinking well maybe that's a way to break the chakra membrane and hear your voice, hello?— I have always thought you one of the most stunningly beautiful women I've ever met. Took a lot of work to get that confession out of me.

Your smile encompasses, that's what I like, to be part of that.

After my father died we moved to Cincinnati from Pineville to be closer to the Grandparents. We lived in a little housing development. I got in trouble. A horse reared at me. There were horses in Cincinnati then.

My candy bars melted and I was stung by wasps. I broke a robin's egg in the nest and I was buried alive by friends. Like that.

I cut my brother's hair with pinking shears. Big Boy in our town was Frisch's. Best burgers ever. Every year the Ohio flooded and we got Flood Break. I got in more trouble.

Then my mother remarried a Nixon clone and my life went into cold storage till I moved to New York at 18. I went to Columbia, now I teach there so, effectively, I have become the guy I used to laugh at.

Then the moth flew in your direction, under your wrist, morphed into bracelet, over your wrist.

Will write the poem while I wait for your response.

I Thought

You would answer

Why I Never Turn Around
—*After Po Chu-I's "Song of the P'i-P'a"*

You were inside the boat.
I was on the shore.
We raised glasses—
No music? That's music!
Hey! Drink, sing—
Dancing music, drinking song!
The blurring river
Soaks the moon.
Separation. What a way
To go—the unspoken word.

Night Day

Another Yawning Morn in the Port of Good News

Impressive, to say the least
One more poem, to say the most
"Good morning. People are boats.
Safe harbor of New York, cling
To the mizzen, the missus and her muezzin
Miss the mezuzah of miscellany..."—It's
A mystery, how sounds become words
And it's a miracle that you still listen
To these scratches somewhere as between
As a head into ears. I am a cat,
Patiently settled at the door to freedom.
I can handle all the freedom, the city
Dishes out anonymity and at day's end
Morning will put on her coat and at
Day's end as she swings open door
I remain sitting. And why not? I am now
With you, no homily. Home. Even
The City that Never Sleeps sometimes
Goes to sleep. Good night.

In the State of the World of Love

It's like cards
There are 52 of them
One for every week of the year

And lovers with amazing hair
And deepsea's pleasure seized
   Tide pasture

Hello, I live in this house
Over the store alone with ghosts
Only are not ghosts they are my life
The first thing is no rules
And the first rule is no love

Gerald Stern Wins the Frost Medal

That party we crashed was not for the weak-hearted or weak-willed—Lordy—it took everything we had in our pouch or seemed to. Our brains were frogs in a lab test and we couldn't stop giggling at the horror cutting into the music or at least the agency you might call it. Someone called the FBI or DEA and we retched on cue which, as you know, can become contagious—an exploding party, all that music on a summer night with no one conducting. And the paddy wagons all lined up, so we whooped on outta there, not avoiding the heart and began working on our love songs and other collaborations.

Good Questions (Dream)

So very carefully unscrewing the turtle shell to reveal the sleeping mouse

Any particular day?
Yes Elizabeth's
Birthday

The door is open and who opened it?
Why didn't "they" close the door after "them"?

The Poem

Thinking of you words
Sail across page
Sail, and land in your arms
The Poem says Hello
Curving a crescent
Sailing back to me

Poem: *Naked Night*

Not trying to impose
To set in motion the secret
The way is pretty durn milky
If you know what I'm saying
Cause I don't you may
Sing this one back to me

       "The Poem that floats
       Its message across
       The land recedes
       To the stars themselves
       The recipients"

         The Poem curves a line to you
       Floats a word back
     That's the way we rock the world

To sleep. In the naked night
The ocean wears a hat

Bob Holman's 343rd Dream

On the veranda at dusk, overlooking the grand lawn, twin miniature ebony pachyderms trumpet across the slate, cross in front of me as the dark simian leaps into my arms:

Holmes/Holman (V/O): *Now I can solve the case!*

Disappearing Into Vision
—For Cecilia Vicuña

I am calling you Abuela

And you are answering Silencio

And next I am just kind of blubbering

Something about Unappreciation

In the Circle of Buzz Bees

And you are looking at me laughing crying

I say something, Hmm? and

Then you say First appreciate

Yourself and I see

Through your crinkly eyes

Blue green yellow

Brown brown brown

You are gone into the smile

That takes me down

Why I even didn't know

I was on mountain!

Almost Caught Fish in Dream

Did, actually.

On string

Just string

No pole.

Could see

Hook

Slide round

Blood oxygen

Gill a rainbow

Trout of considerable appearance

Tugged reeled pulled slid

Then I was called off to do something

And I went there

And it was a while later that I remembered

Fish

Was gone

Labiarynth

Last night underwater swim with Lady O' the Lake

Faraway faraway hmm underwaterfall was a-washin'

The rocks' socks and stones' phones

Twas beyond the cool tractatus, verily kissed among thee

With a nose for a nose and a mouth for a mouth

Together agallop this body illiquid

Ears Sound Good

When day reaches tip-point's slight hesitation

Th'intake of breath, settlin agitation

And the moors' mossy bogwith sheds tarty tear

Thought rises a whalespout—wish I had me an ear

Bob Holman's 371st Dream

Busy fancy hotel shoe store. I need a pair of green shoes. The smartly attractive woman behind the counter points to a pair of green alligator shoes. Clearly, not my style. So she indicates a man up the six steps in the sales area, and she says "Shüss!" which is "shoes" in her accent. The man is older, chubby, sweating, working hard. He indicates the shoes on the wall. Well, there is one nice green shoe in my size—rounded, vaguely clownish. Quite nice, but its mate is blue. The salesman looks exasperated. He will go look for a proper pair. I'm left alone and time goes by and time goes by. And I go back to the woman who points to the croc shoes, shrugs, sort of looks over to the side and when I walk through the door and up the stairs to the back hall there's the salesman in a hallway filled with shoes and shoeboxes. We look through them all. It takes forever. In the end, I don't mind the green and blue pair.

Another Poem

everything happens at once
cops bust in radio says
cops are busting in the wind
ow shatters there is a camel hump
ing down the street wind
delightfully your hair in
my face Captain John Smith is
in Ukraine and no one will ever
sing his epic the same way once

Potato

Once when I was little I knelt before an onion,
Dug my arms into the ground up to my elbows,
And prayed for my fists to turn into potatoes.
The sky was all owls closing in and a sow bug

Waltzed across my eardrum. It went like
This: *dunde sklittle mouse.* A golden melody
Popped and cascaded, I could not tell inside
Outside. Tongue, tongue lay there a luscious
Cucumber. Gasp. No wonder you were surprised,
As I waited for potatoes, as you paraded
Past like a typewriter. I was certainly surprised
When the onion opened and inside was a potato.

Bob Holman's 6,744th Dream

While walking a desolate highway or a mall or a suburban area. See, there's an
airshow going on. A huge plane—four wings? And a large, classic science fiction-
shaped rubber airship coming straight at me. I run, but I can't outrun it. It hits me,
swallows me up, there is an explosion, I'm dead.

Where is my family? People act like nothing's happened. I am dead. I enlist the
parking lot attendant's help to find my car.

Death Is a Boat

(what if

       Death is a

  Boat?)

Make up your mind, BoatDeath!

Life comes at you
    from all its sides

               Water

But
In
The
Middle   you are floating

Bob Holman's 174th and 1/2 Dream: The Broken Watch

A lot's going on at the Club, but as I step out and look at my watch (round white face and thin red hands) &—the hands unsproing! In fact the now single red hand pokes out the casing, like a wire or string, and I pull it out. Upset, I call the watch company to get the address to send it back. It's not that big a deal, the watch repair guy says. Hold onto the hand, click and push the casing and the crystal should pop off. Then double over and knot the string and poke the knot into the little slit in the center of the face, forcing it gently. . . .

Hey wait! I shout into the phone. By now I'm walking through a manufacturing district down by the trains. I don't want to become a watch repairman! I just want to send the watch in and get it fixed!. . . .

By this time I'm walking into a manufacturing/repair building with a window in the wall where you talk to the guys in the shop. A guy behind the window is on the phone, and it's clear from his gesticulations that this is the guy I've been talking to on the phone. I've walked into the watch repair store, although it looks much more industrial, with a shoe-type metal last covered with hardened glue, lots of grease. . . . The guy takes the watch and motions for me to wait inside.

Inside is an apartment which doubles as a childcare center—the kids are just leaving so that the woman whose apartment it is can take over. The place is a drop-in hangout scene for actors, and I see my pal Sal Principato on the TV. Women flirt with me. A guy with no arms leans his shoulder in at me, his way of shaking hands. The decor is spare, the feeling warm, welcoming, clean, collegial. A woman in a beanbag chair beckons. Elizabeth is here somewhere, with the girls. I'm relieved. I can wait without worry.

Without You

I wake, pillow wet 60s funk
Whahoppen. Here I am without you
Oh terrifying night stay dark
Keep out of me sad new world

Inviting 60 poets to birthday yoohoo
I won't show up! the dishes
Set out for meals. Honey come home.
All over the house gray blanket of
Infinite void. I still come around.
Wonder where you went to, all that.
Not so whiney please about the end
Of the world. Mike Tyler told me this one:
Just before the end of the world, the one
Guy leans over to the other and says, Hey,
It's not the end of the world. As I was saying.

Ok, I'm back, it's later. Thoughts rise
Not really—more like they lumber in
From the left, the right, the diagonal
(My personal fave, the lumbering
Diagonal). The pigeons on the awning
Coocoo, the deliveryman ferries
Harryette to school. My mother calls
First thing to remind me to get up, whistle,
Set out the plates. Go into the studio,
Let your hand guide me to paint the end
Of this poem like a little monkey full
Of mischief and surprise run over by red.

In Passing

Mention quickly a lung (one
only) that holds air for entire
planet, well! When the elevator
decides on its own how
many floors, there you go. For
kissing complaints, stand
over there, in the Sadness Line.

When she passed from life, I
remember that last kiss. And
following was a moment of boats
appearing on dry land. They were
Rescue Boats, making headway
against the wind. Just hold on
a bit longer. Just hold on to me.

It Is Night

You are sleeping
The poems are coming
From your dreams
I stay awake
To write them down

I want you to know
When you wake up
I will still be here
A bouquet of poems
To start your day

Hold the Night

You look
just like
you look
but you kiss
like nobody
's business

Later for Now

Bird whistles worms dance
I am your little survivor, Baby.
The delicate penumbra of you
And your family's belief system
Rocks me like the sea, deep
And deadly. Who needs narcotics
When I can make up with you
Or wake up and see you and wake you
Beside me. Wake up wake up
The emergency bellows of heaven
Are crying for a quick Apocalypse
Over your dead body. I will wake you
Because the Jews 30 A.D. wrapped the dying
And when he said the magic poem, up rose
Ol' Lazarus for a last slab of ecstasy.

Plunking on the banjo with you
On my knee. Digging up the jar
We planted in Tennessee.

On Love

They were on love
They were all over it

A jet stream smidge o' paper and
Even a paper clip to hold it all on with

Would their bodies ever quit? Love!
A Handyman's Handywoman's Special

They were equivalent when it came
To sex, burrowing like rabid worms

Seeping like Superman through lead
Surely goodness and mercy will follow

All the days of their life at least
We can turn the page

Where the writer becomes tour guide
For the reader: Look at the Lovers now

Trading male and female, inventing new genders
Call it "May Fail."   Pretty little May Fail

Why do we cluck? On their scrap of paper
In the jetstream with everything

Clipped on—blank here
        Wake up in disrupt sky

To recognize the face of the Other, who,
By breath alone, impregnates, births

Eats up freedom, burning
The sun, shattering planets,

May fail in the freezing emptiness

Dear Morning Light, Dear Visiwind

I hear you hum somewhere deep within.
Pull the covers over. Call it skin.

Morning

You awake
Morning happening
All around you
Dot on map
You are part
Of Morning World
You are in it
This is comforting
The sun entering
Invited or not
The tide on
The sand, same
What else?
Everything
Slowly returning
Positioning
Chairs and rugs
And bedside
Tables. Gray ghosty
Eyes unfocussedy
So focus on nothing
Drift draft. Sleep
Leaves like breath
From someone dying
The idea of
Getting up, out
Of bed, is the thought
That crosses the river
On a raft. What you
Will do is this:
The big pants,
The long rubber coat,

The hard red hat

That covers your neck.

Step into the boots,

Slide down the pole

To the barking dalmatian.

Hop aboard.

Off you go

To fight the fires

Of morning.

It Might Be Lonelier
(Without the Loneliness)

There was a time when and if there is some time left now

I'd just like you to remember we are both alive

      Soon

             Enough

Everything else will happen, or not—in fact

The extreme dailiness of our hour (hello, it is

9:49 AM, 17 July, 2007, on North Grimes

Hill Road) and the

Big blue tranquilizer bobbing on a green flat

In the window's reflection of the dance rests

I am looking and looking and looking

When you say it's ok

To stop looking and

I stop looking

No Allusions to Closeness
of Closeness I Pray

Today is not my birthday. I celebrate anyway. Soon
I'll be thousands, a beach of birthings, a veritable
Ooze. Life out of a toothpaste tube, and a sandwich
Is always there is no there there. But here, with you
As usual, I solder the blu-ray basket onto our helmets
And ride, Sally, ride. It's a Twitter feed with no sub
Scribers, a holdout for holding on. I walk down three
Flights in my Tony Soprano bathrobe to pick up
The last print edition of the New York Times. Except
Someone stole it. Doesn't matter. I can read it on
My tablet, all about you, the things we used to do.

Everything Is Coming Up Roses
Underneath the snow

(SNOW)

unsnownow

I Beg Buddha

To replace my windshield

Dear Elizabeth, Hello

Today would suit you to a T
The T of To and the T in suiT
Makes the O'Day Irish
Promises no legal dispute

I am silly over sad, new geometry
That (ha!) begins with 4 the number
Of Solidity and Death
Gather honey for dinner

Not much has happened since you
24 hours still a day—what's that about?
Greenpeace and Planned Parenthood
Solicitation phoners still call me Mr. Murray

I am happy in a way I didn't know
Happy in dreams you lively
Painting glance my way and
Your Pace show was a hit—sold out!

Not really. The kids would never
Let Douglas sell everything. Just
A taste. What's a taste w/o a T or 2?
Not easy, I'll tell you that

I'll tell you this I'll send it all
I've been remiss—a kiss now
Fast before these 24 pass on
Your day reclaiming tenderness

Song

—for Steve Zeitlin

This morning first thing cat
Jumps on bed howling—it is
Refrigerator/stove and clock/
Radio a-boiling over! OMG I set
Alarm up and went to REAL
Bed, the one where the Dead
Hang out and in at. Cat
Looks at me with those slits
And I transmogrify to siren/
Salt. No more poetry. Only
The sink/window, with
Me waiting, me twitching tail

Movements

List—Spring Cleaning 3/20/10

I am working on Saturday.

I am waiting for my daughter to call to tell me what I am doing.

I am fielding complaints about an organization that I founded, is a service org in a field (spoken word) where there are painfully few resources, and from which I wish to just dive off the fuckin' stage and disappear.

Without bitterness, neither.

I am dealing with the window through which some drunk tossed a rock last night. A thermal window. On the Girls Club side.

I am prepping for 2 classes at Columbia this week because they messed up on the website.

I am way behind on the Welsh but I am mynd yn ôl i'r the didgeridoo.

I have decided to postpone the ayahuasca because I can't stand to have my psychedelic experiences confined to a time line.

I am chairing a panel on Fay Chiang at NYU on Wed.

I finally am reading at the 92nd St Y! Next Sat + Sun! Typically, it's through the Dance Department (a duet with Molissa Fenley) not the Poetry Department.

I am prepping to spend three weeks in Canada in April, reading and performing.

I am having fun with my daughter in town and wish my other daughter were here too.

I am thinking about *The Gas Heart* and think Dagny should set a date for it in LA and get some crazy cast together.

Like James Gandalfini and Sapphire and Claire Danes who are all performing at the Bowery Arts + Science "Hollywood Does Poetry Benefit" on May 2.

I am thinking about your transcendent and down-home (earth) brand of telepathy.

How sweet it is in a blister.

Out (The Window)

Saw so many things
Wanted all of it mine
Busted the glass

The Opening of the Big Museum

It was big, you were lost, the art leads you sure, but you are lost
      In the art
There were colors, all friends & shades, & escalators, saying see
         You later
At the top, there is so much space, blink your eyes reopen, leap
           Into space
Remarkably attenuated, yet forcefully blank, there was nothing you could do
          About it
Many's the time you were forced to draw the blinds behind & stare solely
        At the art
Wandering drifts so many mazed passages & treats of eye flash that you'd stop
       At nothing
Just to see everything was the trick of the day, carousing conflicts of mind &
      Memory
At just the right moment the helicopter would land offering to whisk you up
& away
You wave it on over the broken horizon & keep on searching for what is right
               Before you
The Museum is opening, continually opening, waves opening you, waves
        Opening you

You Can Have My Husband
(But Please Don't Mess with My Man!)

—Elizabeth at 65

Speech Ed Sanders says is bad song we wisp or
Never the brain shall circulate freely midst the air
As when this one night standing precipitously agangling

Might these words sense make back when they would
Of a sudden coast
                    The hurricane of well up
Not a moment too soon not a moment
Too late as when the x-ray hits the fan lots of glass
Everywhere except in Club Bologna Bowery

                    How bland food burps, to remix the scratch
Now it sounds like all new Captain Beefheart
Sounds like your man RL Burnside who wisped
All over the Monkey of Holly Springs which Signifies
Absolutely everything keen red wine note

Suddenly it's very secure
                    Socially that is, except
The Rolling Stones cleave in with that Have you seen your mother
Baby, standing in the shadow? crap and I remember why the Beatles
Always touch me, no matter how many other corpses float by
Speaking of touching, we seem to be doing an inordinate amount
                    Of it in our waking hours, just as
We do an ordinate amount of "it" in our sleeping ones

Try it. You sleep now, and I will watch your elegant form
Crack a bed like a lobster sheds its shell
And you wave to me to come on, fly like a beagle
The very first dog in the Washington (NY) County 2005 Bird Census

So who cares if our friends run into bears, and our enemies spend years
With penguins? We who love the formerly extinct ivory-billed woodpecker, that's who.
After all, it's six months till your income

     Will roll in like Otis's tide,
A herring highball. Your show will redefine art, defy the museum construct and
Still make people think things   green   black   ochre

     Night   pink   punk   clam   dam   spurn   brown   flicker. That's why I
On nights when you're waving I can't wave back. It's totally great watching you
Stir the air. We're talking gesture with no destination. I'm in no hurry

     Vermillion   orange   blue

Poem

Laugh cry moan
At the same time
Is a poem

Impressions

Impression
Deep in paper
A line:
Push me over
Artists clamber
Aboard train

Of Thought
To Nonthought
Just look at it!
He squeals
A ton of cake
On the walls

"Gentle Persuasion"
For all to see
Giving the
Impression that

An Artist
As she stands there
Looking at me
I think about her
Looking at me
Until I stop

She does not
She paints on
I think on
Clearing my throat I ask
How is it going?

She does not respond
I read her hands
The sounds they make
Red yellow blue green
My face my face

Dante's Harmony
In a boat
We take a bath
A trail of clouds
In trousers

The Bar
The mirror is
More like it

The Ball
We are having one

Before the Mirror
Behind her back
There is no me
Wrapped in gold brocade

April Moon
Only it is 2:29 P.M.
In August
And all is not well

Well Among Dunes
Don't whatever
You do look down!
You will see
Me looking up
Pail hits head ouch
Sand trickles from
Your squoozing instep

What Sky?
Look! Look!
The sky gets in here
Keep looking!
Or it will stop. Look!

Signature Gesture
Old Manet has signed his name
Quel horreur gesticulates
A bank clerk madly twirling
His pencil balanced on his nose
Is a lump of shape!

Downhill
Conveniently located
Cemetery bottom of hill

Guess I Figured to Be Done with Desire
That you would take it all with you
Ah! desire for you who took my desire!

Manet in Venice
Blue pants unbuckled
Pour toi, ma Canale Grande!
Thwack thwack
The sound of the brush
On the rolling gondola

They Are Off
How fast can you see how fast
He paints the speed of the horse
Gallop on, my Love
A hoof on the brush in your eye

Moss Monet
Hand-work fluff
Into table gray

As I Was Saying
Monet was painting
Vivid wind

Fleet
Easel down
Canvas up
Paint on
Take pee

While stroking
Sun on beach
Drink beer
Blue umbrella
Salami white chair
Home done
Almost black line

It's a Big Mountain
A little late, village

Occasional Spontaneity
Like now

Horizon
Swam near Étreat
Today went deep
Into what I thought
Was sea
But when
I looked up you
Were looking down
At me framed
Perfectly by sun

Over Here!
Stop me!
Trees are not red!
Is a cry for help!

Celebrating Who Died, Who Is Born
Quicker!

Her Pipe
She'd smoke it
While no one watched

Crazy Hollyhocks
They go insane!
And jump in
The painting
Is way too frogesque

Duck
Poetry quacks alone

Just Stand There
And be twelve
Years old
Forever
Julie

Night
Knocks but
Day doesn't answer

Hanging the Laundry Out to Dry
Waiting for rain

Distance
From expression to impression

Lie on Grass
Lawn motivator

Sunset
If it didn't happen
We could paint it better

We
Reader on horseback
Painter with whip
Walking the other way
Hoping you do not notice

Rooster
Egg balance
My head
Salt

Wouldn't You Know
Alfred Sisley got lost
Painting his way out

The Flood
I forgot
You wrote it
In your painting

Degas, or The Bath
Lean over a little further,
Edgar, or I'll get splashed

In the Chair
How to get more pregnant

One More Secret
Is that the secret
Isn't anymore

Out of Shoes
Into bed

Just Think
A crab on its back
Can teach you to fly

Every Word

In a poem

Is a poem

You Are the Corner of My Eye

You are my rent-a-poem

You are love jungle—Yoyo, hula hoop!

You are my closing costs

My plasma vibrator my single malt

You? You are my Tampa manatee

You are my Occupy

You are an eucalyptus octopus

And a haircut on an autumn day

Also submarine. Surreality check

You *you. . .* ! You YOU *you!*

That's who. The Temple of Shenanigans,

AKA Shenanigan Temple

The complete works. The leftovers

You are what I've been waiting for

And now I'll never wait anymore

Dream baby, you are, and indefatigable,

That, too. And you are the cream in my coffee

And you are the one, and you are my everything

And you are everything I could hope for

And still you are more, and still you keep coming

You are coming like a river, like a torrent

Like an all-day lollipop where every day is today

You are the Castle of Doubt on the Plain of Forgetfulness

You are one more and able to laugh it off

My sunshine, that's what you are

A rocking chair and a band-aid. Violin castanets.

An elusive perfume. You are all history. You are

Breakfast and you are on your way and all

I can do is list, name, and hand out passports
Because you are who you are in a way that is all
Your way and which, as a poet trying to set it down
Failure, I am a failure in that you will always be
Something to me both bedrock and ineluctable
A passion of opposition and an unchecked probity
Of probability and yet a chemical formula not to be
Tested. The Higgs boson, that's it exactly. A gluon.
A ramshackle melody. A forgotten memory that
Never happened and when all is said and done
Actually nothing was said and nothing was done.
That's why I keep writing, endlessly penning, because that's
Who you are and when I stop, Surprise, you are
The surprise, you are the inching to the summit
The chocolate razor, the tadpole's pole and the
Gate to the Fields of the Lord. I sing you praises and
The answer is more like a light fog saxophone, a
Kingdom Come revelation, a hunch that blossoms
To birth a new species. An appointment for lunch
Some nectar in a tube, a pillow. Like the new language you
Are, if I could write that I would, you in a race car
A pendulum, a fire tower, a blimp. A pothole, narcissus
An a capella cantabile, a big bucket of milk. I can run alongside
You but can't keep up with you, your tapdancing
Shadow, your clothing made of earth and spit. But I know you
And when you wish me Happy Birthday I trade it for yours
You not growing old, you everlasting, you infinity you

You

You, on the other hand—
Are out of hand

Maybe a Poem

Maybe a Poem
Would be better

The Snow Covers the Bed
You are the snow
I am the bed

The Sound
Rain in a cup

Things
First
Things
First

Second
Things
Second

Third
Things
Third

The Silence of the Strange People Who Have No Names
Who are we?
We who are strange
Our names are not
What others call us
We have no names
Let us christen ourselves
With each others' names

Trying Very Hard
To get
To work

Only One Eye
And a pillow

Ok Now I Am the Poem
No wonder I have my head
In this pencil sharpener

Tombstone
On my tombstone
It says "Tombstone"

New York, the Rivers
People, the streets
Here to walk
Where you start from
Return to the sun
New York, the rivers

My Mirror
Has you in it

The Moon
Then we walked to the moon
And you said
There's a song in walking

I Am Writing This to You
Long after the chance for you
To be awake to read it
That's the difference

Between emails and poetry
It is so damn late
I don't even know
If I am awake or asleep
I only know I am writing
You

It Is Morning
The sun is late
I wait for light
To see what time it is
The birds are yawning
Quietly and the bees
Are lined up in the hive
There's not much time
To write this poem

Like a Flashlight Beam Across the Sea
Warning the ships from your heart

Now I am writing poems
To explain the poems I wrote
Like the one about how
It's too late
For you to read it
How maybe it's
An email and wahoo who
Knows the difference
A phone call, now
That is different
My ears dance to your voice
But when I say I don't know
Whether I am a sleep
Or a wake

That all I know is I am
Writing
You
And "You" gets its own line
That is because I am not only
Writing *to* You (*to* in italics)
I am "writing You" as in
Conjuring you up
Via the poem
Have you be here
Right here beside me
As I push

        aside

           the covers

Of night and

       sleep

          into you

This Is Just to Say

I am sorry
we didn't have time last night
so sweet and so hot
plums melting midnight

The Poem

Does not miss the paper

3 Songs

Sweet Morning

The battery wore out
The car broke down
More hangnails than
A one-joke clown
The sun
Is my eyeball the moon
My brow I've turned
Into a three-bean cow

Smooth

As you grow on me. Spring
Again, every time I look. Go
Figure, Taina. You jump up,
Your arms are vines' flowering hands.
I watch your little toe gently
Smooth the floor in all the right places.
That's the Earth, your grave.

Ring of Bone

Ring of Bone
Chain of male
Sing alone
Go my bail

Eat my heart in
Meet my cave in
Ever starting
Never came in

Bloody trade-off
What you made of

Rocket Birth Day

O it's a day all right all night snakebite, a wind
smelling of change, a rocket rewinding
to its pad, a body shedding skin
for light, a see-through bone—you
name it. I'll not name it. In the dream

It's now, sleepy
Mexican town and the gang hanging
round broke-down car, turning
corner so sharp you never know

What hits you when lightning strikes, when
the comet settles in like a dusty moth for a landing,
when the submarine rises from the puddle.

I... yi yi. So fast you clip a mirror, big man with
greasy pony tail falls down dead at your foot and
you shot him no you didn't. That is lie! Then what is Truth?
Investigate the body in the autopsy garden, but
it is not until the party where they bring the horse right into the
living room that you are assigned the task of leading
the horse out of the living room, silently acknowledging as party
swirls and raucous ratchet you have been exonerated
hot Mexican day turning cool Utah night breath

Freezes into life you exhale, like birthdays
among friends, when you run slam
into the body you were born in. Passing a shadow
on the stair, was that you or me? I believe it was, is, you
mutter as camera pans slowly round till you are viewing
the cameraman, I mean woman, the true
mother, the eye, not even the eye

It is like seeing
but without the eye

Slam Is the Lighthouse

Slam is the lighthouse for the democratization of art
And the Open Mic is where poetry shines on the world

Something Allen Once Gave Me

You can give money to a beggar,
or not give money to a beggar.

But don't always give money.
And don't always not give money.

What you always do is make eye contact,
acknowledge your mutual connection.

To Pringleize

To force conformity and stick humans in a tube for easier shipping

The Happy Wanderer

I am calming down into
good thing for the system
I'm feeling like all smoothed
out yeah there is a hatchet
in my flask there's thunder in my
knapsack I've learnt how to whistle
like a Jew's heart and keep the beat of my cock
muffled like a fetus

it's all pine needles and crockery
most people don't get it, that's why it's poetry
And when you're done
(sing this one back to me)

Dance

When They Look

At the poems, they mutter,
What is this guy doing?
He is dancing

Stravinsky's Three Pieces
for Clarinet Solo
—*for Michael Drapkin*

I. *Sempre piano e multo tranquillo.* Preferably Clarinet in A.   ♩ = 52

Gotta start somewhere might as well dive in chicken soup
Gulp to health

Such patience the ears have under these circumstances to listen to
Whatever comes their way

Such is beauty. The word *Beauty*. Sound of the word *Beauty*. Whenever
It comes up it reminds me to remember

Future Beauty? Therefore,
Children

Playful multitude physically jumping, the actual chasing of the running,
It's an activity

With no overtimes, except as you grow old fewer to chase more chasing you
That's you back there, returned to child-state

Did you ever notice the slight curve of the parentheses
It's like they want to become a circle

II. Preferably clarinet in A.   ♩ = 168

On the Hey, would you look at that (!)
Marvelous climbing imagination ivy all over
All walls so more room to dance the nice Jewish breakdancing

What fiery beast breathes the moment? Oy!
Where did that come from? Where doest it go? Dust? Hey
Would you look at that look at that one guy says to the other guy
There's the ocean! What? It's a red ocean! Please. The marriage of eye and ear

You talking poetry? As in, "It's all
Poetry"? What are you, *Musician*? It makes no
Sense. Surely we are beyond sense. You falling
Asleep over there? It's not red. What? The ocean?
No. Chicken soup.

III. Preferably clarinet in A.   ♩ = 160

OK everything is in its place and
for the one moving in good thing
to keep out of the way and
dance it follows the
up all night and
it means EVERY
THING
nothing and
going that is the
moving all day and
lease arrangement here as we
another's place luckily leaving a
blank space right where it just was
just keep moving to try to
the birth of
so it stays
word
everything is going to take over one
we do not have a long term
also simply to be moving
music where is it
it flies like

Dancing For Examples

Moon suspended by spider web
Trolling night sky for comet bites
We mosquitos buzzling neighborly
Into flesh of pear

Dancing w/ Destiny

Loneliness is underrated
The sea's evaporated
Wind is full of kites & g-strings
Last scene: fightin' in a bullring
Cut the shit—stream the story
Life is just an allegory
There is something that you told me
Sounded something like "Please hold me"

(after fiddle line)
That says it
Says it all
Cept no fair
Saying it a'tall
The entry fees to the refugees'
Cacophony of sympathy
D-D-d-d-Dancing w/ D-D-Destiny!

(enter w/ fiddle)
Let's unite to keep the freeway free, totally free, an absolute
Freefalling to your arms and calling: don't forget the parachute
A pedigree of pardon me, I'm the MVP of RIP
D-D-d-d-Dancing w/ D-D-Destiny!

Fall Full Fallacy
Fleur de lys flash fantasy
Iron irony from Irony
Blasphemy's eulogy, comedy's tragedy
Now: repeat after me

The maitre d's gotta PhD in repartee
So don't blame me for the bonhomie, Monsieur PeeWee
The honoree had an herbal tea dosed with ecstasy & XYZ
Feel free oui, oui—Finis, emcee! Take the third degree at Waikiki
ASAP BYOB long time no see under lock'n'key
I can't agree to disagree whilst stayin' footloose and fancy free
D-D-d-d-Dancing w/ D-D-Destiny!

(pickin' break—as at top)   2:16
The future's bleak and getting bleaker
Don't forget to tip the speaker
The world is dialin 911
The DON'T WALK sign just changed to YOU BETTER RUN
Hurry, disappear! Back to the Past!
Did you really think the Future was gonna last?

Loneliness is underrated
The sea's evaporated
Wind is full of kites & g-strings
Last scene: fightin' in a bullring
Cut the shit—stream the story
Life is just an allegory
There is something that you told me
Sounded something like "Please hold me"
D-D-d-d-Dancing w/ D-D-Destiny!
(orchestral bullfrog)

You're Beautiful It's True Tango

Up North it's summer so you're here / But here it's winter, ha ha /
Hold me, turn me, curve me, learn me / I'm all yours eight minutes /

[Orchestral Break]

My wife died, she was beautiful / What happens to the mind
Let the night never end never end / I'm all over you and it's over //

Double Beginning

—for Molissa Fenley,
Katie McGreevy,
Cassie Mey
92Y Spring 2010

A Double Beginning

cirrus sans tsurus

Enormous quiet brought you up to date memory
A double beginning
cirrus sans tsurus
Enormous quiet brought you up to date memory

Simplicity when captured isn't
             quite so
                          simple

        Turns into fragments
Fragments fragment
Ferment   Foment   Repent   Cement   Intent
Relent   Hellbent   Per cent   For rent

55

To
   one's
      heart's
         content
            In the dance there are many stillnesses

Level the air and sweep the balance level

I started to make it and then my father died. Study on the subway. A foal jumps, like on TV. The hands placed over the head—a shaking leaf. Things elbowed things outta the way, hey, You! Be able To tell Time like Fela. Ni Knee Jeer EeUh. Nigeria teaches.

Don't Di-a-gon-al *the diagonal as front* ↘

Rely on yourself like you taught me. *It's hard.*

Blessed be the seeds you sow. *Yam eyes.*

Into an overall unity. *Step into a step.* Step step leap into willingness.

The ambience of nonchalance from somewhere else, *fancy pants*
Lying on la playa working hard *step step step* on your nonchalance

                If ya gotta work, it ain't workin
                If ya gotta work, it ain't workin
      Talkin bout Love ya jerk, if ya gotta work, it ain't workin
             & this ends the letter & I hope yr better
                  Half is better than none
         And the one at the end says, Goodbye, my Friend
         Gotta hit the new high before the law gets wind

                                   Gotta hijack a convertible and blow this town
                                   And its underground—gotta make a break
                                   And amend the bend—recapitulate
                                   And capsize the end—a change of perspective
                                   The vision's receptive

Inspiring input put yr foot down   *Step drag step*

Bend and follow   *Bend to bow*

Keep abruption

Too Far Out

                        You gotta go
                        Too far out
                        To bring back
                        The psychedelic boat

Once upon or twice *that's nice*

A hop with you *on it*

Can't help moving *my love around*

Beseech the lack of *too little*

F O R E W A R N E D

Of the stone I say, *It's a stone*

Might *stop*
Pressure *drop*

Or in or on or *on her honor* or over *and out*

Will you wish a song *for this dance*
        placing a piece of body *step*
                incorporate the tender string in
                    the untuned guitar

A spot where you can change
The effortless Groucho and the slow Hangman's Walk into the *mirroir*
O! birds of heavenly delight, Tweet your polyrhythmic antiphonal strophe down on me

When it's pure dance it's pure faith in the balletic leap twirl *right outta there* →
Like a kid on a mission *it exactly*

I can remember the way your body curved into
Mine even as you lay dying there was a mutuality
Of skin I'll never feel again

might stop
hop
might not

might flip
might flop

it's easier
        to follow
it's easier to follow
        what's going on?
it's easier to follow what's going on
                        it's not
                            going on
it's easier to follow what's going on when it's not going on

~~The Double Beginning~~

begins now

Now Begins the Double Beginning!

It's a flop that hips

Might not hop

Might not stop hopping
I hope it stops
        Hop hop hop
            Pressure drop
                Drop drop

The untuned guitar
        incorporates a tender string
                places a piece of body (you wish!)
                    a dance for this song
                        a song for this dance
                          and now a poem for nothing

Out and over and on her
And in her or on her
Or on her honor

The stone says it's a stone
I say I'm a stone
Language is what the stones thought of
When they wanted to dance

A change of perspective—the vision's receptive
Balanced on one finger on a bowling ball
You come to the conclusion as you start to fall:
I'm fallin I'm fallin
I'm fallin fallin fallin
What now? What then?
What's up if not now when
On delay we're on delay
Ándale! Ándale!
It's gettin cold—we're on hold

Step step hands over head a shaking leaf

A hop with you on it

Meet me in the parking lot

Forewarned: the lack of *too little*
Once upon or twice *that's nice*
Abruption! The ambience *from somewhere else*
Nonchalance *lying on la playa*
Inspiring input *put your foot down.* Step *drag* step
Bend. Follow bend *to bow*
Now di-a-gon-al ↘

And now
Your willingness leaps into overall unity. *Step step*
Yam seeds. *Sowing the blessed eyes*
It's hard to rely on myself *like you taught me*
Teaching in Nigeria, the step and the stop step
No jeer iger Nigeria, in *Fela time*
In time, time, *push through air*
To tell time
Elbow out
A shaking leaf

A spot where you can change

The effortless Groucho and the slow Hangman's Walk into the *mirroir*

O! birds of heavenly delight! Tweet your polyrhythmic antiphonal strophe down on me!

A foal jumps, like on TV. Hands placed over the head—shaking leaf. Parking lot

When it's pure dance it's pure faith in the balletic leap twirl right

Outta there → → → → → → → → → → → → → → → → kid on a mission

cirrus sans tsurus

Enormous quiet brings you up to date memory

Share it like an orange

Sectioned like a daisy

Petals like a cross-town Motown

Parking lot

Pick it up

From another

Not quite there

But hear

The End

Helicopter Flower Flower Helicopter

That spring
was unlike any
other time I've
ever experienced
full of the chaos of
existence, meeting strangers
who turned out to be
the lovers of former lovers,
taking a job that immediately
turned into a whole different thing,
where my skills were actually used
and I was actually paid for it.

In the morning,
one cup of coffee
and a cigarette
and I had the whole
Times crossword done.

I'd watch the City
come to life as if
it were a painting
that animated
with the sun.

The noise went
from silence
to deafening
in one single long
crescendo, a delirious
inexorable Dance of Evolutionary
Participation, if not Understanding.

It was all done
in the doing.

I wouldn't go
so far as to call it joy
but it certainly did
smack of life
lived at full intensity,
two trees bending
in a hurricane,
totally set
loose and yet
fully grounded.
A *dance*.

I found myself
repeating certain
phrases when certain
images approached:

Twisting The Sky
Setting Fire To Ocean
Lightning Strikes Under Water

Finally I admitted
I was in love with K
the animals
who had been waiting
alongside the highway
watched my gyrations
as if I were their keeper

who watches
who sees
who knows
who cares
who believes
who introduces
who follows
who wants to know
who couldn't care less
who understands
who starts over
who balances
who jumps
who forgets
who dashes

who realizes

who raps

who taps

who says get lost

who touches herself

who appreciates the repetition

who has inherent diversity

who wears her body on the inside

who takes you for a ride

who can't help it

who gives up

who reimagines

who flies

who lies

who brings it whole cloth

who carouses

who stays up

who comes together

who appreciates the last drop

who winks

who blinks

who finds out

who can't believe it

who loves

who touches

who sleeps

who shares

who journeys

who incarcerates the imagination

who luckily meets another

who swings about

who terrifies

who twists

who incinerates

who lights
who puts out
who justifies
who guarantees
who leaves it well enough alone
who can't stop
who puts best foot forward
who swirls
who resounds
who flips around and over
who stands tall
who stands still
who is alone
who gets ahold of sky
who insinuates the beat
who doesn't know
who lifts
who dives
who dries
who dies
who branches
who cries
who ever shall see
who ever is aware
who ever stands before you
in constant movement shall
create a world that
is yours alone
who enjoys
and who sings
and who brushes
and who latches
who brings rings
and who swims in air

and breathes dance
who cantilevers and takes
it all in
who stands forever
finally leaping through the window of faith

In Church Dancing

No chords heard, the balustrade full of confident spires. The stained
Glass a-blazing, the monks' vivid carousel carousing in the vaults
Like water in a cyclone jar, twirling the frankincense like a helicopter
Of flowers. Irises. Peonies. Petals flashingly floating by. Total
Immersion in the sacred laws, reveling in Absolute Freedom as defined
By that movement which embraces God as the Body and never the other
Way round, and then the Other Way Round and About and Did you hear
The plainsong chant that built on a climax of union—a lost note becoming
The dance itself, can you hear the dance with your eyes now Helicopter
Flower the church engulfed in Actual Flames of Salvation, burning
Burning yet ever whole, unscathed, a testament of faith a vision of profound
Balanced perfection—Stasis Absolute—fragmenting into Molecular
Particularization of Eternal Inevitability—Only the Vision Of The Faithful
Shall emerge, a new Understanding so full of light that drowning is
A natural state and to ascend is to comprehend the glow and blaze
Life assumes, the Last Water, normalcy finally exchanged for
The physicalization of faith adjudicating itself, one to one to one, a tree of
Music rushing to sea to return a wave

STEP

—for Molissa Fenley
Atlantic Center for the Arts

STEP aside someone is speaking
AND they only have one tongue
SAUTÉED in absinthe windows open
MANgrove swamp Florida
CITRUS coconut candy chachacha!

SMOOTH the floor, if you don't
MIND leaping above the floor
YOU are still
YOU are still there
YOU are still there between ceiling and floor
SUSPENDED in slight pause
FLOATING the way a poem
FLOATS just over page, hovers there
TURNS change out, kind of like you are a gay bird
AND have to live alone because no one will let you get married

SO—fuck marriage, right?
AND live with the one you love who is
ALWAYS on the diagonal ↗ (at least in my experience)
THE way a green bouncing by will suddenly eye you
AND you decide okay okay
WE'LL spend the rest of our lives together

PUT a tattoo in there, that will
MAKE the perfect body perfecter
ON the other hand which you must
ALWAYS wear on your other arm
I'M talking (as ever)

I'm talking! I'm talking!

I'm talking talking talking!

What now

What then

What's up

If not now when

What's next

On the way

On the way?

Ándale!

On delay?

We're on delay?

It's getting cold

We're on hold?

Gotta stop

Take a break

Take a breather

Break a breath

Or an either

Or an or, or, or. . . .

YOU can stop now and let your
PHANTOM limb move parallel parallel
AND now—CHANGE!

It's the CHANGE part where eight
Attractive dancers are hopping around
Whoopsie-Doodle!

W   h   o

o

p

s   *D*

i   e   o

o

d   l   e

In interesting forms and then, *W*

                    W   h
                          o o
        p   s   i   e
D   o   e,   just slip down, reinventing
        o   d   l

What—Well, I learned this from Edwin Denby
Great poet/dance CRRRITIC
Inventor of the Rear End of the Horse
In Orson Welles' fabled WPA
Restaging of Feydeau's *Horse Eats Hat*

                              So you could see CHANGE
                        As being all these dancer prancers are first
                The neighing bray of the gorgeous windstrewn mane

                              o

                        o

                              p

                        s

        CHANGE to *Wh*   D   l
                              e   d   e the rear end
                        i   o

                              o

                Of the horse a kind of feet plant torso-butt twist,
                Much more of course attractive than w   o   r   d   s

Which brings up w   o   r   d   s, okay, I know
While waiting for the dance to go on and on
One can only hope forever
Provoking all manner of bird tree ocean star speck can opener imagery

But over all I think you'll have to admit it's the W   O   R   D   S
That are in all probability the ass end of the H   O   R   S   E

Part 2,741

Outside Original leg a leg a right ↘ left diagonal ↖ space hold

   u   r

T   n step step bigger
        ☞ Left ☞ left ☞ left right ☞ and a right ☞ a
       W   o put the stage under these delightful feet?
        h

She so turnip green original side slide
Downstage pulls them (feet) right off
Stage here comes light a life FORCE
      A life BOAT
           A LIFE magazine
               A "Life Poem"
                     We are the Original People (OP)

Dancing is what walking used to be *and a hip turn*
Your body goes right where *your leg was*
And this part is just *running around like your life depends on it*
                    And doesn't it?

               Yes, dear Poemlistener Danceseer
                                 ?

[*performance only*] How did you get yourself into this? ?

                                   ?

It's quite the unwilling suspension of disbelief I tell you
      To rest ass(end of horse)sured of *that* that!

                                  That's not right

                                  Not Right

There's too much of a feeling of generic seriousness
Going on here, walking long the beach
You come across a piece of driftwood carved
Like a sculpture and it's snowing and
Your partner is dying and through the tears and
Snow you are painting a picture of all this
Right   Especially the driftwood sculpture
Or maybe you really did transform
Into a deer, the way Pan did
In order to disappear into the poem
You can win the girl, especially if you are the girl
Accent right left and the horse you
Rode in on Whoaaaaa!
And it's the first time you make love
But this time you go real slow
And you get your clothes off with plenty of time

Turn corner of space

On Top of Transition

Hmm.
And again, _Hmm._

All this gesture comes at you and then settles
So that maybe you don't wear any shoes at all
Or maybe, you think, okay, you're right,
I'll wear one shoe—the downstage leg ↘
So I know which stage IS downstage
And left left dazzling twirl and drills
The earth, it's a gusher, folks, it's transporting
Mountain stream veritable waterfall of movement and face

71

Faces face and turn burns twister chachachanging bean garden

Of course needs weeding so—weed it!

Now you open up the body like you open

An egg carton can and then you open that egg

It's the 10th Position of the Everlasting Apocalypse

The minute you start to start that way start

To flower that way turn that way

Dance opens into Mouth of Love the whole thing falls apart

                                            o

                                        o

                                            p

                                      h

                                        s

Crisp drip veggie barbecue RELIGION the *W*

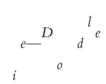

Of the funky transportative chimney puff all remember!

Original People! (OP!)

Dancers are the Original People

Take the original path to the original home

There are many many many ways to get there

It's kind of amazing that you actually get there

But you will. You will get there under the structure with signals in it.

You may want to do this part holding hands

And singing an old song as the snow comes down

Too bad you can't I must say Understand you must!

That you cannot hold

Hands. You cannot sing you forgot the words and
You are tone deaf. And you can't go
Home, ever, again. You must
Dance the earth's giant dance.

Gazelles, antelopes, why not walking on your hands
The clankety clunk of the rackety garbage truck pulling
Up to the dumpster in the middle of the night
And as for the raccoon that is sitting on the tree limb taking it all in
Yes of course, it is her poem.
A simple arabesque, yes, can do
Repeat, not so simple, one more time, that's it
Certainly must be someone's birthday, nice cup
Of tea, and a promise to look each other up
As soon as we get back home to our computers
Logon Snapchat

Which means get home
The luxury of which is never quite realizable
But always works, wearing those work clothes
And matador joy through the motions for
Motion's sake, walking through the unpoison ivy
Kick brush kick brush slide slide slide
All it takes is everything, your all
And the rain stops suddenly just as you walk off stage
And sit down beside me as I join
The dancers and the poem can end like this
In someone's ears, in someone else's poem
In the Land of a Thousand Dancers dancing a Thousand Dances Land

For Everybody in the World Dancing

—for Sarah Skaggs

We are not gathered somewhere else today

Full frontal wave commentary form from

The Perfect Stranger standing perfectly still perfectly beside perfectly you

It's just one of those days when love falls in love with love and the garden

Blossoms orange hammer lilac

I see you on the sidewalk with a bread pole and a red boat

I see you in the library with your beneficent peagreen coat

And whenever the seed drops a hint we pick it back up a tender gesture

As if to say dance day to night then dance the night away

What happens when Ear marries Eye is a gorgeous simply

Gorgeous wedding whispers Tongue to Neck, officiated over

By Nose, all working together, the Dance of the Face Wedding: if only

The Face had Legs, she

Dances with her Ears, I mean, Ears, can you walk on them?

And hears through her Eyebrows, sound shimmers

Into Skin a river of meaning interrupt this powerful image with a tiny

Can you wait a moment while the Skin next to you does its little dance too

Can you hear it saying It's summer's end, as if things ended

What if you could marry the air? and children everywhere

Foolish buildings stare back as if they owned the earth give me a break

And a clue of too many anxious belabored hell if I know

Light bursts forth and people, real ones like you

And the fruit vendor and the hot dog guy and small private booths

Or sites in the corners and the

Horse, horse knows its way around

Everybody in the world knows couldn't even give over the Time

Of day so busy, with the impossibility of joy

Feet upside down thoughts

Patting rhythm rhythm never forgot

Of being home wherever, like in a Park on 42nd,

The time Time stopped

And we kept dancing

Ornettes

The Perfection of Time

Unresolve

Free grammar

Poke angels

I was saying what can I say I was saying

What I said I was saying to say

Backbeat leading

Something ground up thinking laid gentle derail

Amongst the top truth I'd-a yodel so swept

Filched magnificent resurrection and kept it a-beatin' throb throb

What was the yield patty ain't a mister take two

Come back here to where it is once belong

Branded squander factory for fools

2

Gobbling up silence useta be's

Dance eternity

I climbs out put that boat down

Water sinks below air, breathe volcano yell

Yellow springs binge just to tell the true take

Bury me with her and you and him and take us over carry by caravan

Love me like lies and never try excuse me lily disappear who

Singe since yes sir today since little closet

Closest tomb—lemme break it down you

Talking

When I'm talking there's something I have to tell you but since I don't know what you're getting I have to keep on saying what I'm saying

Sound 2

       Sound's just formation
             Meaning head connect
  Never something but now
     achieve Unrecognizability
                     What's it tells you it can cannot
A taped CD found in Japan
           The be ur end
             Bliss please
       While waiting
         For   bourgeoisie's   ecstatic   syntheses
Of
    all
        our
    petite

Sound

Sound's just information
What's in your head meaning

Never but now connect
What's it tell you something

Unrecognizable ur: a tape, CD,
That cannot be found in Japan it can

Bliss please
While waiting

For ecstatic syntheses
Of all our petite bourgeoisies

Signals

Importantnottoputupwithrepititionintheformofinspiration

To stay finding signals

      Structures with signals in them

Cash the Last Pass for Me

Playing Ideas

Thank you for prying

From voice to dramatic things

Creative sounds happen

At this vary moment

Saying a Moment

Happen to it

  Wanting

      That's moment

             A saying

             Automatically you're saying

                  You're what

                      Express you

                         When?

The Other Side of What You Just Heard

When you express what you're saying you're automatically saying a moment that's wanting it to happen

Like an Oboe

I'd peel open onion oboe the big eye

Keep that tread retreading threat of a thread.

Bowling for archangels, I'm ear. Flute cello,

15th century verb you. A delicate circle

Of sphered intent—take the one on the bottom.

Fall on top of your earthquake.

Back to Earth with Eric Dolphy

With all due respect to your boyfriend
I am back

The Sadness Is in the Sound It Is not the Sound

To resolve is to kill the third

Idyllic Umbilic

I and her dance
Salty violin garlicky panther
Lampshade dust collector
Mighty fine dust
Over that particular lightbulb
You were saying
A French horn memory? Ha.
Well, there was a revolution
Before you were born, too

Pause for Commercial Identuformation of Continuing What You Were Saying Barbecue

The violin which had kept the backyard mowed
Now wants to reflect the stained glass window's white
Careful drinking audacious driving to get another drink
The sea is locatable to the other

Oboe Hop!

This place consumes musicians—can be
Counted on to release bassoon from dogcage, John.
The noted note prefers collection connections

Architecture in Swung Motion

And still never happens. Church bell now
Ornette wills an umbrella (roof? naw) and
Sure enough it is raining.
What what
Is what.
Umberto Ornetto.   Will tango
Snare escape consequences?
Always end at the beginning A

If You Dig This It Doesn't Matter It's Wrong

Morning. Trumpets open on west.
The strings pull the sun along from the east
The winds are all over that thing

Home On The Road

Pappa Was A Peddler
(Kentucky Yiddish Story)

Papa and Bubby
Landed in Brooklyn
Dispatched to Harlan

Schlepped pots and pans
No English but price tags
Tell the story

A Jew in New York

Like everybody else, I wasn't a Jew
Until I came to New York. In Portland, OR,
The other day, a young Latina asked me
If I were Jewyorican. Papa and Bubby
Came from Ukraine, landed in Brooklyn,
Settled in Harlan, KY, and named my father
Benjamin Franklin. My mother, the offspring
Of a coalminer, married Ben, the only Jew
In town. He didn't last. Ma remarried.
In kindergarten, in Cincinnati, instead
Of moving to the afternoon session second
Semester, I stayed in Morning and changed

My name. This is the year 5755. In Chinese
It is Year of the Dog. I just learned that the time

Between Rosh Hashanah and Yom Kippur
Are the Days of Awe. Moody and gray,
With dashes of absolute clarity, I love
These days. Cleansing summer's sweat from the streets
Of New York, I always think of the year beginning in
September. "That's when school starts." A holdover
from Youth. This year, for the first time, I think
It's the real New Year, and I am a real Jew.
A real Jew, and a real coalminer, too.

Village

I live in the Village
Not just any Village
Not just every Village
Where the City
Becomes a Village
That's my Village
Where the intercontinental
Becomes the neighborly experiential
That's my Village
Uptown Downtown Lowdown Notown
That's the place that's Home Sweet Home Town
The Village is where I live

Jane Jacobs is my patron saint
She lived it with her apron paint
Stuff she saw she made you see
The definition of reality
A mix, a mess, a mishegoss
Trees in cement, mental floss
Ideas drip from a faucet
Grew up in a bedroom closet

Circumambulate these concrete paths
Tantric trails evanesce the globe
Centered on this Village energy rocket
Simple pulse of living here
All lands and all peoples living here
Behind blinking windows of stacked buildings
Population froths in undulating syncopation
Utopic and grand, elegantly funked and plastered
Mighty Squat Humanness
The Village where I live

Friendship

First day of fall feels like first day of fall
Something right with the world standing on ATM line
West 12th Village morning brittle breeze tiny man in overcoat
In front of me pivots, remarks
       Be-you-*tea*-full day
       Day of Beauty I allow
The World in the Wind
Stops for a red light
Crisp money spits from machine, hot
Off the press, twenties salt the air, take flight
       Like to visit? he asks, hopeful eyebrows
I follow his hat up stairs through locks
Cramped musty, a crowd of paintings, golden
Light says "Time" infusing his face
The Hudson swims low in the sun
We huddle round the samovar
He brought
From Russia

Bone china cup
        For you
        Glass tea
For him

Our faces intermingle in the silver curves
The tea he serves is the *tea* in Beautiful

Inside the Synagogue Is Mars, Inside Mars Is Your Apartment

—A poem for the opening of Angel Orensanz's installation,
"Flying NASA Lab," 1/15/04 at Orensanz Synagogue

You land on Mars and you're never coming back
It looks like Earth because you come from Earth
Hello Mars, this is Flying NASA's Lab Report from
Rover Spirit beaming pictures' pride explosions
You land you are free but it's not land you land on

It's chutzpah art! enriched detritus! covered in penguin dust!
It's Chinese Yiddish. No, Yiddish Chinese.
And It of course is Not It, but
A Red Carpet to the Stars, a Panoply
Canopy of Sky Snowing Plaster Memory

It, meanwhile, is just chilling, circling in space ballet
A woman, man, manikin in a spacesuit bikini
Recycle Mars trash art. I live in New York, Mars
My kinda planet. The fire extinguisher hisses
Chemical temple soup. The ladder

Raises an eyebrow to the sun. Look down, there's everything!
Everything is what Mars is, and it looks exactly
Like your apartment! A synapse leaps here, goodbye
Poem to reader, hello! Send me a postcard
From Mars, sign it Angel. Driftwood drifts by

Hollywood leftovers—Movieland
Caterers' lonely folding chairs now a mountain
On the plains of Mars, as Martian ants
Parade balance tightrope strings
Weaving the whole thing together

Big Iron snowshoes. Luckily it snowed
A crater rocked over, that is our mission
We call it the Lower East Side, twelve
Candles in a row. The melt is on!
Inside the artist's mind, his

Hair. No! Hair goes on outside, drifting over
Angel's forehead reflected in a black disk
That rescues the symmetry of light
What the hell is that poet doing? What
Is he talking about? What's the meaning

Of meaning? What's the purpose
Of purpose? What's the use?
Can I use it? It feels so good
To refuse it. Refuse to be burnt out
Refuse to interpret. Refuse to move.

Refuse to refuse. Refuse to shut up.
Inside the synagogue is Mars
Inside Mars is your apartment
And behind the door, an old woman
Is waving you in. Come in, she says. Please.

The trip to Mars is but a jaunt, a *passagiata*.
Walk in art, walk in artist's mind. Walk
In poem. Walk in the synagogue of your apartment.
Strolling past Mars, you keep going.
Goodbye, you wave. Goodbye which means Hello.

On Mars

The other day Hal mentioned
We were living on Mars
"We've been here all along," he said
Bijou was pulling us along,
And Minter was nowhere to be seen
"Well, what's the difference between
 Earth and Mars, then?" I asked
"They are the same," Hal said,
Bending over to use the plastic bag
"It's just that on Earth, Bijou can't talk"
"Right-o," said Bijou
Minter dropped in
On her flying saucer then
"Bagels all around!" she said

14 Street

It can happen anywhere
But not on 14th

All the way home and back
Loopity loopity thru the variegated scoopity
Forever Alley

You can walk all day, hustle gristle, light up the night
Get belch'd out from Con Ed Generating Plant
Skirt Alphabet City and The Low East
True Downtowner's never been above it

On to Union Square and the bulk of it
Nowheresville linearity with a return ticket to You Never Left
Bumper to bumper cars, blaring busses, papaya stand
Totality banality—incarceration of flickering stares

The only street that's got its own subway, so wherever you are
You're just a few steps from the Underworld
From the Mighty D to the Meat Market

Essential delineator
Edge of the edgy
Culminator of solitude

Ravages of whatever poem you sought to ascend
Thoroughly burrowing throwaway thoroughfare

Hymn O'Hernia! Ode Inauspicious!
14th! Belt of the Borough
The steady slow drip
NYC's IV

A Real Stage and Like a Punk Festival or Something Cool and Loud Salsa

Dear Shirley,

This is your first morning in New York and this poem lasts as long as life
   And the Twin Towers are burning in the sky

and the Chrysler Building is keening and

The Empire State all gray and stolid is etching its shadow
              in the neverending breakfast
     we call sky

    Of course all the New York poets are already out writing poems
Walt and Frank haven't even gone to bed yet

and we are all feting Elizabeth Bishop who
     coincidentally
       and believe me
           everything
in New York is a coincidence, breathing and walking
       even this poem!
     and your first being here on the very day (here we
go again!) Senorita Bishop turns
     like a left turn right into
        100 years old,
sing!
    So if this poem is as long as life and if Elizabeth B. is 100
What does it mean

   What does it mean is what we always ask poems
       but since they are already out ahead of us
they only have time to briefly turn around
       in their kickass gym clothing and
   fashion week accessories
      and shout, Whatever!

and tumble on directly and digitally into a future
where the Poetry Project, Nuyorican and Bowery Poetry Club
    where Poets House, Poetry Society and the Academy and

Max Fish and all other holy spots like Taylor Mead's bathtub, Frank O'Hara's haircut
        and John Giorno's mouth and Anne Waldman's energy closet

all sit up with Langston Hughes and Allen Ginsberg and Frank Lima, Julia de Burgos

and rest assured

        (That's the motto of the day, "Rest Assured")

                as your yellow taxi turns the boogie-woogie criss-
crossstreets into Mondrian,
        as MOMA becomes Yo Momma, as Harlem beckons home
And Cai and I will read at the Club at 6pm
        and who knows who will show up

                Which is the other thing for sure, that who
will know who, as I know you, as the poem
        is now out of sight, and to read it you must catch it

which means you write it

        like Eileen Myles says
and like Ellison Glenn and Beau Sia say
                        Write it in the sky
        which is now prepping lunch and your table is ready
                        oh so ready
                            to spin

Tompkins Square Pastorale

Pigeons peck poems on pavement.
Ants crawl in code up paint-cracked bench.
My people sprawl in vowels, yawn a couple

Hiphop lines. Sun ball boils. Sudden rain runs
Steam locomotive. *It is raining*. But what is
It? The grass
      under the sidewalk
                    shakes
Its greeny head.

Rain
—for Danny O'Neil

How I love
To stand
In the driving rain
Blowing my horn
At the entrance
To the Holland Tunnel

Nickname

The Bowery Poetry Club's nickname is
"Black Hole Into Which Everything Disappears"
(And becomes a poem)

Canceling Gig Last Minute
Bowery Poetry Club

For the Club it means bartenders
Get no tips on drinks they don't ring
Sound guy sits around,
Rent maws wide open—no ka-ching!

Occupy

I wanted to change the world but it was Occupied

So I opened up my window and tried

To catch a breeze in my baseball glove

But the breeze was overtaxed already

From the kites held aloft looking back at us

With spy drones and jawbones and maitre'd clones

So I just went down to Wall Street, That's All Street

Yes it's All Sweet with a Brawl Beat of Raw Meat

And when we Occupy the Zone of the Capitalist Nose Cone

You can bet we're aimin to be framin demands on the sidewalk

Blitz toe rag slag down to Zuccotti Park

Bring your own consciousness and some rolling papers

Unleash your sense of humor on some deadly pedants

And let the spirit invigorate your sorry consciousness

Yes U.S., you need a jolt! Coffee's gone weak at the knees

And the train's run out of steam and in black and white you dream

Of a land that promises everything and then laughs atcha behind yr back

Watch out, America! You'll soon be Occupied

By pies that are growing grander with each incoming tide

Cause there's no outsourcing the Truth

And the magnificent battering ram of wealth on screen

Keeps driving the responsible into a surrealist scene

Where the Mommy and the Daddy got no job but it's ok

Cause they pay and they pay but where's the wallet today

And it's got the wings of a vulture and the tale

Of the epic story of how you were born

You were born a twin where one of you had to win
And the one who won is carted off to learn the gun
And the losers are stacked in cardboard shacks
And we'll Occupy and we'll Occupy
Till the day we die we die

Duskus Interruptus: Boulder, Colorado

"If only the Whole
World could be like this!"
Writes my Naropa student
In her notebook
As we toss beer empties
Into the dumpster
At Varsity Townhouses
And scan the horizon
For Noncaucasians

U.S. Poet Delegation Kolkata Book Fair 2008

Stock market dives into Ganges! Holes crack Holy Sky!
U.S. Poets enter Kolkata! Nothing but words.
Everything is words!
Words every thing
Words greeting breath
Words transforming political
Word's history roaming, finding itself—Surprise Future!
How about more words? Flow flower full force!

Words' roads leading—follow complexities of Heart
Dance aortic pleasure, rush ventricular whoosh
Lost? Read map to me—it's a Poem!
A gift of imperfect understanding

U.S. Poet Delegation, Kolkata Book Fair 2008

Honk!

Taxi Ride with Joy Harjo,
Kolkata Airport to Hotel Landmark

Hurling black taxi into mad river chaos!
Rickshaws! Rickshaw humans! Bicycle rickshaws!
Moped-driven rickshaw surreys, fringe atop! Insane bicyclists!
Honest-to-Nandi Sacred Cow crossing unhurriedly! All traffic
Dead stop Ganges! Candy-colored trucks, eyes painted
Next to headlights, ward off accidents! Multicolored signs
On back of every truck—
     PLEASE BLOW HORN!
    OK, all together –
     HONK!
Individual build constant crescendo eternity bleat Honk! Honk!!

Honk! As you start to pass, there are no lanes in traffic river
Honk! Ok, come on
Honk! Thanks, I am now coming, dangerously close
Honk! I see you, I like it this way, c'mon
Honk! Ok me too! Sort of got by you! And I wish to long-
    Hooooooooooooooooonk! you
Honk! Fantastic! I shall staccato-burst Honkonkonk as drone-
    Honnnnnnnnnnnnnk
Honk! Goodbye! Good Honking you

Honk! at cars parked too close together
Honk! at bicycles going in the same direction on other side of the road
Honk! at stop signs but please "Do Not Stop"

Honk! at rickshaws as they pedal dosas' tin containers to market, to hungry
        masses awaiting lunch curries
Honk! at planes overhead—will they Honk! back?
Make sure to Honk! as passengers exit from any vehicle
Honk! at gas stations "you never know"
Write poem about When NOT to Honk!

Build car around horn Honk!
Honk! Holy Mother India
Every Honk! a prayer to Krishna!
As you approach a fly over

Honk! As you fly over
Honk! As you take fly-over over fly-over
Honk! Lullaby, Howrah Bridge
Honk! Salt Lake with no lake

Honk! Khaligat big toe in Ganges changes direction
Honk! Chinatown! where did the Chinese people go?
Honk! Book Fair! biggest in the world
Honk! Universities! learning is a sport
Honk! Poets Coffee House ghosts of Ginsberg and Sunil and Hungry Poets
Hello! Subbodh and Gary!

Honk! Wet diaper smell
Honk! Green pollution
Honk! Smear leaf—paan!
Honk! If you have horn
Honk! If you do not have horn

And now on back of (honk!ing) truck, Joy reads the words:

        Please Use Horn
        HORN DEEN

Muskogee musician poet
Nods with understanding authority
Gingerly opens case
Pulls out saxophone, alto ebony
Places reed in mouth
Breathes fire through instrument
Emerging sounds serenade symphony
Cascade cacophony
    Kolkata Concerto in B Flat-Tire Major

H   O   N   K!

Charlie Listens
—Charlie Mangulda

Put earbud in west ear
Other earbud in east ear
Charlie listens

Clapsticks, didj, now your voice
Recorded yesterday, Mt. Borredale,
In Amurdak, you're the Last Speaker
Hear? Your voice doesn't sound so good
You sang good, but the recording was no good
Could you sing now, Charlie, please?
Charlie nods. Charlie listens

Clapsticks, didj, now your voice, please—Now
Charlie listens
Now Charlie listens
OK Charlie, we need you to sing Now

Charlie nods and listens
Now Charlie listens
Cue Charlie—listens

Get Cousin Jamesy
Jamesy tells Charlie
Charlie listens

Get headphone splitter
Jamesy puts on headphones
Charlie and Jamesy listen
Clapsticks, didj, Charlie's voice
Jamesy sings a little
Jamesy looks at Charlie
Charlie looks at Jamesy
OK? Charlie listens

OK, Jamesy now speaks Iwaidja with Charlie
OK, Charlie listens, Charlie nods
OK Jamesy looks at Charlie
OK clapsticks in fingers
OK Charlie listens, didj
OK now. Now Charlie sings
Ma barang!

At the Wailing Wall

Sun bakes rock
Rock makes wall
Walls make Jerusalem

Walk into the tear   that is the cloud
A memory from the past   you never lived
The words dripping   black honey

Clogwyni o Llyn

Gwau gyda nodwydd cyflym
     Ac agorodd gyda fflaim
Cadarn-droed y grisiau i fyny clogyn gwenithfaen
     Rhincian glaw rhwymo,, pwyso i mewn môr

Bydd y bydd tân yn rhad ac am ddim ac yn pasio iddo
     Naid gyflym cyn y sioe cysgod
Nawr mae'n priffordd super i roc a rôl
     Traed dapio allan gân y gerdd

Cliffs of Llyn

Knit with a rapid needle
     And unraveled with a scalpel
Sure-footed steps up the granite cape
     Gnashing rain, lashed, leaning into sea

Free will and fire will overtake him
     Leap fast before the shadow show
Now it's a super highway to rock'n'roll
     Feet tap out poem's song

Remnants Performance
(Life, Liberty, Pursuit of Poetry)

—Groningen (Cafe Verla)   10/19/98   3:21 A.M.

kiwi egg toilet paper nest floor after-gig Groningen

to be floor to have seen from below and supported

to have been through under all to have remained

poets their mouths milling grinding spewing sieving

time getting stuck between mind-sharp incisors' husks

light-biters heavy-spitters raked naked oratorians

ejaculating pojizzarama bang garbage lids' wrenches

walls melt under-sound wheelbarrows scrape cerebrum

nailing meaning music arrow flight snip kite string

kiwi egg toilet paper nest floor after-gig Groningen

solid flicker gaping totality eke syllable crust gasp

one big dive off the white apartment building waterfall

jet of language trail to Sirius Dogstar visiting recording

scientific data interbreeding with alien populace returning

everybody pregnant all in a single glance remember

to breathe it's a good thing spilling every idea into sheer

invention children pop out of your suitcase and sit there

Poetry Reading in the Jungle

—After Popo Dada

Not sure what I'm doing here in tropical forest in this canoe

I seem to be moving in tiny increments, all around

trees sounds and flights, rustles screeches and blips…

The fact is I'm asleep. The truth is I'm lost.

My memory full of last night's poems right here

amidst crackles howls trills and banshee wails.

Like the one about the crocodiles that were living in an underwater house

where we were drinking rum, some of the guys

smoking to frighten the mosquitoes,

and believe me it's hard to smoke underwater.

So then they started in on poems,

poems of distant lands, countries at war, green

as Ireland, cold as Argentina, hot as Baghdada,

as Cairo, "It's quite warm here," the Irish poet noted.

"In fact the heat makes it impossible to move, thus

(poets actually say "thus") I drink the day away

in this chair." "That's not so much," the Cuban poet

was heard to mutter. And nobody knows what happened later,

where the poets went. All I do is sit in this canoe as it swishes

round in darkness at 3 a.m. . . . No one is paddling.

I have no paddle. Maybe I'm part of the poem

the Irish guy is still writing, having a beer,

trying to bear up in the tropical sun.

A poem that will be read to us very soon,

a poem he does not stop writing.

Reality

There are eight original ideas
One for every day of the week
Little by little it occurs to you
The extra idea will begin
Another week full of fucking ideas
And when that happens take
A breather between richer and poorer
Between snowball and thirst
Between the linen sheets that cover us
And when they drop us in the tomb
The last idea is called "Poem"

Poem

La Pura Vida is late & everybody's pissed off
Waiting like a lemon on a windowsill
Every glass is crying
Every mango is terrified
What's the matter, asks Music
It's English, says Water
As a bird drops a blossom
Two gardenias for your hair

Trump's Mystic Doorway

The ancestors of the
Are discussing the exiles of a
With the lost children of an

Black Star Night
in the Middle of Life

It's a black star night in the center of town
Don't look—the ocean cheats the clown

O Baby O

Tequila shots 1 A.M. 68 years later
Slide a wedding dress through your mouth
Darling, who's loving you now?

So Much Depends Upon a
Red Wheelbarrow Glazed With
Rainwater Beside the White Chickens

I'm not sitting here
At the Observatory
      In San Jose, Costa Rica

Listening to Frank Baez
"The Marilyn Monroe
      of Santo Domingo"

Read a poem
Drinking an Imperiale
      Writing this poem

The Secret of Life

If it's secret
It's not life

Life in the Open

Turn off the light
Read me the poem
That writes itself

One Day in Limón

Today is one day in Limón
Tomorrow is another
The next day, you'd never guess
Is another day followed by
The next. Today someone asked me
What day it was
I said, "It's one day in Limón"
They looked at me like I was crazy
"This whole place is crazy," I replied
"Come back tomorrow and it's the same thing!"

Group Poem
—International Poetry Festival Costa Rica 2008

I feel lonely and I don't know why
Maybe because I am many in one?
Luvion de Aurouras Infinitas
Estalla en la frontera mas proxima
En los phegles del atousdecer
Sitting by a bottle of whiskey
Me gustas quando abres tu puerta y salen los monos congos que guardas en tu ropero
An onfuil a teanga fein y Costa Rica?
Ver verde velar al verde
La noche termina, empieza

(Written in classical Arabic and guaranteed untranslatable)

Toda la nide se va en ales que regresan

And whatever else, it's snowing, remember

When truth spoke for itself, you poets

Y mis ojos te mizaron como si el taeo fiuit pasasae de nuevo por mi casa

The Poet

Yes, I'm a poet

Born in the sea

Learned to talk all by myself

Never listened to no one

Always had ways with words

Sticking out of my mouth

Shrapnel from grenade

Had a lover once

Who held my tongue in her mouth

Just to get me to quiet down

I loved her then. Love her now.

Part of the job description is to be in love

To fall in love all the time

So I've been busy falling in love with her since we met

And I'm not finished yet

Today I held her tongue for a long while

She's looking at me with her Sun and her Moon

Words slip between us

Meaningful   Improper   Skyluna

Lemon library of gears

Lone whistle coyote

Guitar with two missing strings

So the poet came out of the North

With a tragic look on his face

You listen with all your ears

I speak with all my mouths
Let's do it alphabetically tonight
Big bald dictionary written on the city line
One foot in a basket of eels
The other a refulgent cigar
What's for breakfast?
Silence
An egg of silence

I Am

Not

Poets of Medellín

The Mountain is escaping the City!
House after House races after it.
This cannot be happening.

The Mountain lopes along
Making its way to the Sun.
The Houses are composting themselves.

The Mountain is now big as the Sun.
The Houses are Sunspots. No one
Can possibly live here. But we do,
We poets of Medellín.

Centrally Park

The public bed, a
            shopper's beach

Statue river traffic
            turns you into uneasy hero
Tall saddled, horse cantering
                        circles 'pon circles

It's a fast shot of the races
            an all-green urge
                        Could you—why don't you—
turn off the TV of the world?

                        Sit on this bench beside this stranger
            go on and question, sigh, fan and linger
It's a noise show slow-down
With an idiot's boom-box suddenly blossoming

            into a carousel of characters
My children, my children, step right in
            The zoo is open and the bars in front of you
Are nothing but slow shadows

                        Top level of the tour bus lifts off
            New Cyclone at Coney
The Sun turns from Frank O'Hara
            Begins conversing with you

            Barreling ahead on skeletal schedule
With everybody everybody everybody
            talking to everybody everybody everybody else
                        on single universal cell phone
      World walking to the beat of
The symphony of the street love

Grandly and Centrally

Grandly! and Centrally!
Locally universally
Typically cryptically
Prototriumphantly

You come here to go there
Literally everywhere
Hip trippin Flip floatin
No me-and-ering

Grandly! and Centrally!
Methodically centrifugally
Take you where ya wanna be
Multidirectional simultaneity

Zipping Higgs boson, Reality's gluon
The station sits formidably. Maddeningly. Meddlesomely.
The ratchety manifest. The voluminous steamer chest.
The rivets and pivots and divots of rush.

A trip to the seashore—Picnic-In-A-Box
Pickles, gefilte fish, a schmear and some lox
Fried chicken, varenykys, collards and grits
Hot dogs and frogs legs don't dish the dish

Tamales, pasteles
Spaghetti and gravy
Call in the Navy!
More hot sauce and quick
And the goat's still unroasted
And the bagel untoasted
And the toddler is gurgling glee

At the constellation ceiling
The gods still are stealing
Glances at humans as they bump, dodge, careen

You cross time with space, cross space with time
Just so you can rhyme "sublime" with "sublime"
And the blizzardin' tickets keep fallin' from Outer Outer space
And Sun Ra is smiling through the Conductor's face
And this glorious moment can't keep up with the human race

Cause yr waltzing in Grand Central with the Love of yr Life
A single accordion is playing yr life
The moment is stuck and recycles again
Just because it stops doesn't mean that it ends

So keep lining up, Chumps
Facebook the rumps
Lined up before you
In sweltering clumps

Maybe this is your stop
Maybe this is where it ends
Someone passes you getting on
For them it begins

For you're going Somewhere.
Somehow. Sometime.
And the place you will land
You don't know with whom you will dine

But some Strega, Picayunes,
And a ghost on the dunes
Your family's tunes
They toast randomly
For it's Grandly So Grandly
And everso Centrally
Let's call it a Century!
Grand Central Station!

Walking Brooklyn Bridge

This stunning stand,

Lifting, rocketing towards sun!

Icarus' dream, span

Pointing empty sky,

Where Towers had been

The day the clouds rolled back

To allow a little light in here

Manahatta touches bridge's landing

Police get educated here! The sick enter all doors here!

Trinity Church spire tilty above—

Below foaming, probing. Here the city erects

Patrol car waits like a cat. Brooklyn shyly beckons. Love ends.

Chinese father in a light running suit, his daughter in fashionable mixed plaids

Manhattan Bridge searches north, crossing like an acrobat

And south then to Verrazano, stretched below glass caverns of Wall

Tall ships now a tourist attraction! South Street Seaport Om!

Lay the words on you! Sprinkle organic jimmies!

East River is inviting—ah! blue green this morning, twinkling

Anti-suicide fence runs alongside, equidistant, no problem

All downtown spread out crazy quilt southwards

Thrum thunder, cranking autos

A bench! who sits? who writes?

Helicopters hover Governor's Island

Uptown blocked by project's tiff, Empire State peeks between

Manhattan Bridge looming o'er FDR attracts small buzzing plane

Two dogs, their masters in matching red berets

And here at last long cables swoop rough roped steel

Anchored through hand-cut boardwalk gaudy streetlamps rusting

Handrails change the ballast

Here the crossing wires, the famous photo of workers spread across Dada sky

Pedestrians right   Bicycles left   Walt centers

Electric line, illuminating globes parting opera night
Flag atop Arabic arch, negative space
First cell phone of the day!

Oh Manahatta, Tow! Spooling over proprietary river, opening tower shields!
14,000 miles of wire rope, from East River to Timbuktu, Roebling's great invention
How he got the job! Noted on plaques! Official plaques!
The official garbage can! for official garbage! New York, recycle!
And now, officially—Brooklyn!

Williamsburg glints through Manhattan Bridge web
Brooklyn marries Queens! Sea wharves mounting movement
River of calm, Staten Island, her Ferry setting out

Tourists with video cameras   Cell phone after cell phone
Some in heavy winter coats this blazing Sunday, fall's first day
Others in shorts and tee shirts insist global warming is a daily occurrence

Cables slide back to rest   Midpoint balance
Ah, more official benches!   Why not sit here, see you face to face?
Write a poem, hymn. . . .
Sailboat salt   motorboat sugar   Circle Line bracken   ferry silt
Commerce slow this Sunday morn. . . .
I approach you, these thoughts of you
Begin slight descent—again the rockets, the Arabian sights
Looming elegance, sheer geometry stone
Someone has left a note and a rose
Korean soldiers in gold pea coats

Watchtower announces itself
Familiar Earth rushes up, greets us!
Parents point   children don't look   surly teens with hands dug in

Tension packed, lifts, shot off, Brooklyn gestures, "Come on in!"
New park borders river
Ferry landing with no ferry—Wah!

Exit signs for BQE, land lashes out

The trees, the autumn trees of Cadman

Over our shoulder, the other bridges come to rest in congruent conjunction

Oblivious baby in oversized stroller, an hour's extra sleep today

The smells of spice, rot and salt, gasoline

Anti-suicide fence finally gives pause, gratitude and stress

Sweeps a moment of choice

Walk up swirling splitting subway to sky, river to stars

I turn, walk Walt home

Praise!

Papa Susso Christmas Praise Poem
(He Is Still and Always Will Be Muslim,
Not to Worry)

Papa Susso, Griot of Griots!
Knows Allah personally and when he sings
We hear Allah's voice

Papa, you are force for Good in the World!
The Sun is Papa's brother and the Moon is Papa's sister
And all the Stars are his wives and children

So at Christmas (and all other Christian holidays)
And at Eid (and all other Muslim holidays)
And at Hannakuh (and all other Jewish holidays)

And at all other holidays of all other religions
We sing Praises to Papa Susso for bringing us God
And the Stars and Sun and Moon all together—

(Written while Papa sings us to sleep
Looking at the Milky Way
Over _Sotuma Sere_, aka Hometown Village)

Praise Poem World Heavyweight Championship Poetry Bout 2000

OPENUP!!
Hope-ope-hopen-up
Open up!

Here join in the salmonfull

> luminous animal

> > nightbesotted anti-school

Where the Audience reigns

> not to mention *participates*
> but also to mention *rain*

This is it The Big One
World Heavyweight Championship Poetry Bout 2000
As you've heard mentioned previously, Mr Rabbit & Mr Bryant
Having so eloquently hyperbolically informed us about

HmmHmm **HmmHmm**

HmmHmm HmmHmm

So we might as well get started

> *(Haven't we already started?)*

The Poems started long ago when the first Poets crept into Taos under cover of darkness to burn the light off Pilar & run away to join the Circus—The Poetry Circus! All for a taste of Annie MacNaughton's hot sweet coffee at Mexican Bob (Amalio Madueño)'s Poetry Camp. . .

Poetry to celebrate

    participate

        & cultivate

           at any rate perpetuate

Tonight in the Camisa Room Sagebrush Inn I'm talkin zip code 87571

At this point yr probably wondering what is this guy into

    Nuff already with the intro

    Let's get on with the poemmmmmmmmmmm

        HmmHmm   **HmmHmm**

     HmmHmm   HmmHmm

So I hope it won't be upsetting

        If I say I'm Bob Holman

        & what you're hearing *is* my first poem

This is A Praise Poem for the Bout

        For poetry

           For poets

              For us

(That's where I start. We are all poets (I just thought I'd mention that

(Personally I'm just back from Africa (I've been studying with a griot (a keeper of
the oral traditions (Alhaji Papa Bunka Susso's teaching me how music and poetry
originated as one (& it's part of the poet's job description to inaugurate events with
a Praise Poem celebrating those who make it happen.)))))))

So Hear now the Praises!

     Of the places

        & dayses

          & amazes Taosentric

Generous folk in high place(s) (6997' elevation)

Now charitable bountiful munificent & liberal
Are not things we talk about these days
Without embarrassment considerable

Ya ya I've borrowed this praise chant
From the Family Dembélé

      Of the Djibasso region

         Of Burkina Faso

& if I keep going on like this
  you'll have a first hand experience
    of why the oral tradition
      probably died out in the first place

Or maybe tonight we'll survive it
Revive it make it live it pass it on
& all leave this Bout humming

    HmmHmm   **HmmHmm**

   HmmHmm   HmmHmm

So I guess I can stop this singing
(That is if you call this "singing"
Though personally I just call it
"Reading the Poem!")

HERE WE GO!

Gary Glazner, Margaret Victor, Juliette Torrez & James, Rich Forrester, Abraham Smith, Bob Fullerton his new wife Robin (they met at Burning Man) & their 4-month-old, Aila Mariposa,

Back at the camp, my buddy Joyce Star Beader & Adam, hi Brandon, Julep, hi Dove! Diane, Catherine, Carlos Torterrici, not to mention Aaron Yamaguchi & camera David Hong,

Anya, Carla, Barbara, Susan, Matt at the door, Haridass, Chairman Brigette (my dancing partner) *"I hope this is crrazy!"*

We got Bill & Linda on sound—thank you! Kenn Rodriguez, Esther Griego, Jim Navé, Tamra Nichol, Danny Solis, Sonia Faher—congrats! DJ Murph, Genoa, Oryen, Rachel, Tessie, ElizabethLorennaSusanne, Rick, Diane & Ryland—buy books from their bookstore!

How bout the Youth Slam?! Lettering in poetry at Taos High?! Erin Bad Hand, Sexy Sherman Cortes, My Man Juan Concha, Anna, "Taos! Seattle! Taos Seattle!"

Tiwa, Keres, Lakota in the house, Philip the Rappazappa, Scott & Dale Harris (thanks for the juniper salve for my burn!),

Lisa Gill (I will love you forever!), Judith Hill, Jan I love yr hot tub, Donna Snyder, Jesus Guzman, Miriam Sagan, Mitch Reyes, Robert Masterson, Joan Longhe, Laurien Cook, Joanne Young and Marilene MM, Laurie, Melissa, Ian, Matthew, Gwendolyn, Nyla the Snake Woman, Star & Rima & Julia Roberts you look great on yr big blue tractor,

The visiting Slammers! Noel Franklin, Corby, David Hwang, Paula Friedrich, Big Poppa E & Spam & Scott who left Matthew John Connelley in Minneapolis, Gee Murray Thomas!

Rudolfo Anaya, Joy Harjo, Margaret Randall, Tony Maras, Patricia Smith and the other Patricia Smith, John Crawford, Arthur Sze, Carol Muldau,

Denise Chavez, Jimmy Baca, Levi Romero, Mark Rudd who I went to college with—hey, back in the day!

Maria Leyba, Kell Robertson on his big horse, Keith Wilson, Denise Chavez (I owe her), Besmilr Brigham in her Alzheimer's, Lee Bartlett, Alex Jacobs (I produced his video),

Lana Norta, Aaron Bradley, Margerita Ortega, Dennis at the General Store who gave me the Open Palm Good Luck Stone, & dear 12-year-old poet of the future Grace, goodnight Gracie!

I'm part of this with Sherman, with John Trudell, Jerry & Diane Rothenberg, Ishmael Reed, Nanao Sato, the poetry firm of Jacobus Simmons & MacAdams, the list goes on&on&on-on-y-on

& for those who think this is just one big kiss-ass poem I say

Praise to You, Too

This is Praise Poem for All of Us

Let's praise Max Finstein
He was nuttin but a poet
His spirit soars on
As the Trophy of the Bout

This Tribe's grown too damn big
These lights are too damn dim
Besides they only give me ten minutes
For each of my poems
(5? omagod I must be over already?!)

In Africa the griots get paid off by cash on the forehead
Here we do it with applause
Think of each clap
                    Closing a gap
                              bringing us together
                                        I'll take the rap

There's a ton more names to mention
                              most of them are Indian
So I think I'll cede the floor
                         to my most esteemed friend and Champeen
Besides I have sit down & write my next poem
So…

A ROUND OF THUNDER
(each clap
        closing the gap)

T h u n d e r   f o r   t h e   W o n d e r
Praisers,
        Stargazers,
              Trailblazers,
                    Hell-raisers,
                         Applause for us all
                              Who answer the call

Poema de Alabanza
para Pablo Neruda

—for Songs of Love & Despair: A Tribute to Pablo Neruda,
World Financial Center, April 15, 2009

O sing, Poet! Or not, your voice croaking with wonder
Where the magic at? You were not born!

In the paper scraps and cigarette ash and paper cups squashed and mashed
In the gravel and glass bits, in the leaf crumbs and in the blue poles and orange peels
A world where Neruda was never born or where he was born Pablo Neruda
And changed his name to Neftali Ricardo Reyes Basoalto

El Vate, the Seer! Your eyes distinguish the Domain of Poetry stretched like garters
Around the thickest live thighs pedaling away in the great
Make Love on a Bicycle Race to the end of the Poem
Where Revolution lifts and sings the pure blood of sunset,
The tragic rush of night by night, the neon terror of moonlight
Only you can see by it, *el Vate*, O Seer!

Neruda, All praise your pistol of words, *la pistola de las palabras,*
Here, where the body is spice, salt and sweat! Why, one day the road
Itself started walking!
Luckily Pablo was there. Stop, Road! he cried,
How can I go about my business if you won't stay still! And the Road answered
And Neruda got it all down, that is his poem about artichokes, five I love yous,
And socks, don't forget! and the way the sea wave broke
Over his eyebrow became his "Ode to Whitman," and left the critics
Strangled, and *If only Madonna and Julia Roberts would read*
My poems! the exhausted ghost of Neruda was heard
Muttering out there in a heap inventing God

Whose hurricane? Yours, Maestro Whose abyss? Yours
Remember the time you said

You were bored of it, bored of being a man. We

Were on our way to the Bowery Poetry Club, and dropped by the tailor's

You like so much over on Essex Street. Your pants weren't ready!

That was an explosion right there, and then we walked past

The barber shop and you got a whiff and it was like all hell broke loose

Could we have a little vacation from things, please? you roared

No more boulders, no shirts or gardens, insane asylums, merch or contact lenses,

Elevators, I was writing it all down furiously, THIS IS A POEM I was saying to the passersby,

All of whom were either frightened or pretending nothing was going on,

This is New York after all! you bellowed, an elephant calf on Broadway, transformed

From human skin into the beast that uses its nose for a ladle—*Grab me!*

You informed me of my destiny, *and swing aboard! Your damn Praise Poem*

Is not worth one lash of my eye, one corpuscle from my bleeding tongue.

Give me a full woman, you continued, now just trumpeting, and I know

The mosquitoes that were Buzzling around your ear were in love

With your protein-saturated blood

What does it mean, a Poem of Praise for a poet

For whom the Universe is a Poem of Praise?

This is a vial of poison then, crimson lime and foamy,

A wind-whipped umbrella, poking out cats' eyes,

And God's toothpick, and of course the old reliable belly-button

(*El ombligo*) (not my own), *un poco de problema...*

NO HAY PROBLEMA

¡Problema!

¡Aquí!

¡Yo tengo uno! Más de uno, de hecho un puñado de ellos.

Mi vida es un enorme problema hecho de una millonada de pequeños problemas.

¡Ayúdame problema! ¡Aquí! ¡Ahora mismo!

¡No es problema encontrar un problema! Ven aquí.

Los sacamos del saco, problemas, problemas, problemas.

¿Cómo te atreves a decirme, "Qué no hay problemas"? ¿Bromeas?

¡Problemas, problemas, problemas!

NO PROBLEM
Problem!
Over here!
I got one! More than one, actually, a whole batch of them!
My Life is actually one Big Problem made of a gazillion tiny ones.
Help! Problem! Over here! Right this way!
No problem to find problem! come on over here.
We got em by the sack, problems, problems, problems.
How dare you tell me, "No problem." Are you kidding?
Problem! Problem! Problem!

But meanwhile, aiee, there is no meanwhile!
The lush mannerisms of the palm world, the relentless wings of the sea
Call back the melting earth—as we take the Poet's hand, as he grabs the pen,
Together we swing the curves to loops and dots to crossings as the Poem emerges
Praise the Poem, dancing into being! Praise the words, translations of all things!
Praise all things, manifestations of words! Praise Pablo Neruda! Poet of All Things All
Love All Words' Worlds! Praise Pablo Neruda as pen dives to translate the word

Neruda!

On the Street Named Pedro Pietri

On the most amazing day you were born and you were died

We was waiting for you everywhere and you surprised us

By showing up everywhere else

Where once were bottles now only bottlecaps hang in mid-joint

Waiting for the air to turn into red wine and cheeseburgers

And the bottlecaps without bottles will be redeemed

At the Church of Our Lady of Tomatoes for five bucks apiece

Now that you have your own street named after you

Maybe they will get you a car

But you know you need the OK

Of the Latin Insomniacs Motorcycle Gang Without Motorcycles

To set up toll booths at both ends of the block

So that once you pay to get in

You can also pay to get out

Unless the toll booth keeper is at the other end

Of the one way street that never ends

And you get to stay forever

In the bodega that doesn't sell anything

Because it is made out of loose joints and condoms

And the only way you can get in is to smoke your way in

And screw your way out

And when you drive your black helicopter over the street that has your name

And see the great balls of fire that are being lit up in your name

And the outrageous acrobatic screwing that is going on in your name

You may very well want to change your name

But you can still pick up that notebook that you left in the telephone booth that time

And make your escape into the day where it is always night

And laugh at the poets who try to make sense

Of the fact that a street has your name on it

But you will never walk on it

Because you are too busy writing a new subway

That runs directly under the street that has your name

Where you are on an Uptown train going Downtown

And you name it "Speedo"

Nia! Imani! Kuja Jakaleah!

—for Sekou Sundiata, "the new blue Sekou"

And let me tell you 'bout whatever it was Sekou was talking about the everlasting
life last time well it lasts and lasts till you look

it up in The Googlepedia and shore enuff that's tough

That's right that's rough

What's wrong The Song

comes at last and says to the Poem:

"Why the waterwaterwater? The water sure is cold down there

And all so dark in the deep in the deep deep sleep

Where the last thought you keep

is a keeper, a sleeper, a morning glory creeper

WHAT YOU DREAM UP, IS DEEPER THAN WHAT YOU KNOW

And meanwhile down under the bridge that train keeps coming

Ghost Train coming to Hauptbanhoff—

you get on but you can't get off

It's all your mind, you may be lost but you can always find

that everlasting Sign at Last that lasts and lasts

Outlasts the Past you cannot ignore

We've been through this before the good ol *je t'adore*

How come you make me go to Kwanzaa, Grandpa?

Don't call me Grandpa. Well, what'm I s'pozta call you then?

Robert?! Call me Slick and lay it on thick and deeper than D

And freer than free

Throw yr hands up in the air

You know, like you just don't care

And Mandela left Harlem on a rickshaw chainsaw

which leaves him now you know Now's the new Now Lo-down

Now with a wow ow on a death bed, been there whoops done did still doin oh
    shit and why a bed he said

Why not a chair a lair a zen den w/ a dollop of gin

A grinnin' beginnin' everlastin' life with a friend

That's my kind of Last. Look! you took a look where you take

a last look around where you'll be found somebodybodybody told him

Told him off like a mouthful of Mouth Almighty

So you go on ahead now, around where'd they go

And here in the parking lot, that'd be a good place to park for a while

Maybe it's a Monopoly game played for a fiery gain and Free Parkin' that old Ghost Train

And Craig and I were on that bridge too, weren't you

121

That's the bridge that bridges dirges and all that too you digiridoo

And what'd they say and what'd she say
And what'd we say and and what'd you say
When he said that said that said that we said that you said
Hey ververever lastinlastinlastinlastin
Everlastin life like Kurt said when they stopped the kora it was just short of Andorra
and Wayne went to Providence his reverence was his reference
and what 's that got to do with the do wit the dadadodada I ask you now and then
and now and then is my next of kin which is why the skin sticks so hard to the kiss
you miss you find

That and

Nia! Imani! Kuja Jakaleah!

Tato's Hat
—Tato Laviera

Tato's hat
Is where it's at
One cool gato
That is that

Loisaida peak and brim
Tato's hat out on a limb
What you say you see you been
You lost your hat, so follow him

Now Tato's on the further shore
Swimming? Flying? No more chore
His books won't shut up, they never dies
Tato's palabras to the wise
So wake up, Bro, and sing a hymn

Or be a him, be us, be them
La caretta's on the go
Where it stops, nobody know

He sang his dreams with blinding beams
Las avenidas was his scene
Don't mess with Tato was the word
He wrote the word, that's what I heard

So don't tell me that Tato's dead
I think his hat slipped down your head
Inside the brim, inside his skin
TATO LAVIERA! Live like him

Lester Afflick   10/1/00

huddling poets inside dark perfect sunday fall warm
day outside tribes we gather inside lester late the late
lester in the middle of a poem that doesn't quite start
is scratched out xxxs doesn't quite end what you
thought what you taught what you suspired
stood for your ground some soaring rarely—cynic
died of poverty died of overdose of love died
of loneliness camaraderie red wine too
too much poetry not enough vegetables
always thought lester one of the smartest guys
i know always loved between him and farris
cannon the crew something about us snapped
into place into focus even high today he'd be
here wouldn't be anywhere else cept dying young
afflick a fleck ash afflicted with life in the middle
xxxs to get it write it keeps it going for you lester
for all of us here huddling poets inside dark perfect

Hell and High Water
Steve Cannon Praise Poem

So Steve is on his couch and

The world is his pychophysishrink

And he is buzzin and noozlin

Which is his way of "writing"

Pontificate ash falling on page writing

Down everything everybody's saying "seeing-eye poet"

Every damn time they say it

It's like Joe Gould and if you don't know

Who Joe Gould is then go Google motherfucker

Go find out who Joseph Mitchell was while you're at it

Then read more New Yorker than the cartoons dammit

The Oral History of the Universe

Is World's Longest Book is a

Hoax!

Of course don't bother with the damn New Yorker poems it's like the way

We don't mind calling up Wynton and asking him to play a benefit for Tribes

But I'll be damnation in a barrel of pasteles

If I'd ever not know him the way Butch Morris

Would drop by and John Farris and then

When Zoe lit the damn building like a cigarette

And Baraka, he'd drop by and Ish would and all them guys

And there he'd be

The Professor

Sitting there slouched there reclining

With a cigarette like the time Zoe

Lit that building up like a torch a church a fireworks Hell or High Water kind of place

The second line in Nawlins kind of like the parade

That we did to reopen the Nuyorican from Miky's ashes

And don't ever let that one slip by when they count the years those doors were open
And forging the signature on the NYSCA apps all that shit

All that shit went down like Tribes goes on
Come Hell or High Water The Last Poets
Sekou and of course Jayne Cortez
I thought I'd never see the day Jayne be crying
Because 6 months after her Serpent Tail book was published
They took it out of print now who ever thought that not me
Or my name's not Steve Cannon and of course it's not it's Everett
You'd never hear that kind of thing happen at Fly By Night Press
Cause we already said we don't pay our bills cause we fly by night

Which is to say—We All Blind!
And just as soon as David Hammons drops by
To sign the couch and the piece we've got it all in storage
Sign it! Sign it! Come Hell or High Water that's a million dollars right there
The only admittedly blind art dealer in New York has spoken!
Or should I say, heckled! Yes, come Hell or High Water
The Only Paid Heckler in New York

Bang 1947–2011

bob sad news
billy bang passed
away last night

on a train
in a taxi
on the subway

in bed
passed out on the sidewalk
dead

I remember
everything
like a song
that won't stop
like a radio in the night
a single sound

billy bang billy
bang billy bang
on the fiddle and soul
your black violin
your jazz walking in

to the room
where we wait
for the plane

for the tour bus
on the corner
whistling at play
in the fields
of the lord

Newly Revived From Mummy-State! Saturnians Will Now Party Eternally

—For the
Ra
of Sun
(0-00)
and Herman Blount (1904–1993)

Sound spritz tweaks Thru-Space

    News blitz leaves a you face

        True Beyond

    I'm gonna sit right down and stand right back up

  And write myself a symphony

Sliding a backwards S train whistle

      We are not born again

      We never got born

         All we be is Be

Sun lost

  In Sun

  Becomes Sun

This is not this but WATCH IT as IT becomes THAT

        Shriek is blat squish pero rass the blastoff

That old manuscript of yours that sat on that same spot on the same shelf where you
    left it So Long long ago?

Now's the time it picks to tumble a waterfall to the arkestra stand sit and dance
    around

We wit whip the turbanned trombone dirge

King Squawk of the Evidence Invisible

                                                    The jury
                                              The jury may
                                        The jury may still
                                  The jury may still be
                            The jury may still be out
        But you are always in

If I Were To Throw My Money

If I were to throw all my money into anything
I'd throw my money into the Deaf community
If I were to throw my money anywhere
I'd throw it into ASL

Because the future of the species is immune
To all preaching science normalcy and the silence
Of these moments is best spoken to
By the liveliness of the Deaf community

Oh in the silence
You hear a heart drum
You hear your ears pull
Air towards semicircular cilia

But in the gesture
Of the measure
Of the pasture
Take this detour

ASL'll lead you
Past the pasture
To the Gate where
You will hear there

So take my money

Take my tongue

Take my breath

And see it fly

Listen to the Deaf Community

Listen to ASL Poetry

The whirr o' meaning

Coming up for air

Walk together to the riverside

Making small talk sign by sign

The Body's speaking now, hush

Listen with ecstatic eyes

Not So Coincidentally

—(Poem written at Flora's 80th for her "Coat of Honor."
Title from Adam's opening remarks.
Inspiration from Elizabeth.)

Just in case you're wondering

Where you came in and where you got off

And who was there in the meantime, it was

The Last Day of Summer and the First Day of

Now Everybody Knows How Old You Are

It was Flora's Birthday Wild Party and Vija

Sings "You're no good

               You're no good

                  You're no good

You're no good   You're no good"

As if rock'n'roll were just being invented

Which is true enough

            All things being unequal

Which is what we're here to celebrate –

The reflexivity utility of one woman's imagination
Flora, who rocks so serenely
                    You are welcome to stand
You are ordered to dance because Flora's flowering
Flow rules! breaking all rules

                    And bringing together together
For you and yours
                    Who are us

An urgent patience and
    The emergency of art

                    Calling the roll of images

    Cracking open the world everborn

        Happy is the Birthday of Flora 80

    The art of art

Praise Poem James Siena

The Mystery of Existence
Tape measure

Everything's Going (to be ok)
Wanna ruler
When ya go
Darker

The First Two
Colors vanish
Hoy hoy hoy

Deeeeeelaid Gratification
They're going to get
What we want

They Cannot Vanish
They do though
Tonight I'll be
Staying here
With you

This Position. Wrong.
A measuring mistake on my part.
Art cares. I don't care.

Prop That Little Baby Up and Move It
Might
As
Well
Cut
Another

Not Human
Too early

Nothing Doing Pink
Doing pink faith the lip
Airy all going believe
Light optical allusiveory

Color Blind
You can put that in there if you want

Earl Gray
It's not that you see everything gray
It's that you see the wrong color
James Siena

Stroked Grid
Vertorizon much–much more fucked up
See your eyes stick to the globs damn

Look up close wash it down no no unfuck
The peppermint grappa holy diagonal pave
Estral zingy sharp reverb lays the string
Container no air let it be out of proportion
All kept to through blue few knew too crude
Lay off on it there it vanished awright
Can't believe ok the equal value o shit now

Ecocyclicadic Gardensile
Little tiny printing press with instructions typed writer

Do Not Nothing
You too fill up the environment
And the of course die

My Mother
Was very determined
You have a great
Product you should
Go to Mommy's lawyer

Noiseless
"Pretty Noisy" by Satie

Nesting Connected
Get out of this nest!

Post-Mugging
Adirondack valve

Battery
In the middle a spark
On the fringe a flange
In the spark a dark
In the dark a flake

Upside Down Devil
Rightside Down Dog Town
Hey, Joe where ya goin
With that sharp bubble there

Not Exactly Straight
Get used to it

Not Exactly Straight
Exactly

Not Exactly Starlight
Use your eyes

Not Exactly Straight
You got two of 'em don't you?

Not Exactly Straight
Between the eyes

Not Exactly Straight
Close enough for a hard-on

Not Exactly Straight
More

Not Exactly Straight
And on the level

Not Exactly Straight
Continue on like this till you get it straight

Not Exactly Straight
O yeah I see what you mean

Not Exactly Straight
But straight ne'er the less

Not Exactly Straight
I learned the trick in the second grade
How to draw a straight line
Not straight

Drawing (after Logarithm)
The ship successfully separates from the storm
By the ocean
After the lighthouse successfully

Off Register
Can't won't don't
Look at that

Other Mind Thought You
Everything darker now make
Extinguish to distinguish

Blue Corner (Poem)
Logic does not work with the same Other

Lattice (Poem)
Other Mind thought you

Boustrophedonic
As the plow follows the ox
Round the mountain here she
Comes here she comes

Praise Alex Katz

with practically no show of emotion

Where it's at
Finds Alex Katz
Trees and birds
Jolting verbs
A nose that shows
A mountain's trim

When in doubt
Katz is Out
He's in the bend
He's out again
Emotion blends
Red tongue and gin

Clipping clouds
Eye slits crowds
Sun sits growls
Friend or fowl
Jeweled teeth trowel
Shoveled wows
Portraiture in fortitude
Scaled in epic solitude
Katz' flat humor interlude
Narcissus' bitchin' pulchritude
Festive slick flat certitude
Coordinated amplitude
Can't match Master's attitude

All day art eyes fill and flow
Flowers, showers round they go
The gallery can't hold it all
They smoke and joke out in the hall

Turn to the City that they see
With nothing doing irony
They want blue he gives 'em black
Colors sharpened whack whack

It's like a film
The mountain's trim
Features abstract
Just her, just him
Ada's lips kiss sapphire sheen
Sacrificed to god's machine
Is where it's at
Finds Alex Katz

Jean-Michel Basquiat
"The Melting Point of Ice"

HEAR ART WORDS
ART WORDS HEAR
WORDS HEAR ART
HEAR WORDS ART
ART HEAR WORDS
WORDS ART HEAR

The Samo Samo Copyrighted Copyrighted

© ©

Writ

up

down

overer

underer

innerer

outerer

                              wonderer

                              asunderer

                              blunderer

                               flavory

                               savory

                             loquacious

                             beloveder

                              squisher

recovered ladder to latter lend a hander

   ~~crossed~~-out means To read Do read

                    Jean-Michel Basquiat
                  cause célèbre case fúnebre

Celebrate the Host

Shoot up Ghost

Chase Dragon 'round room

Exit thru Entry Wound

Shutting up shooting up straighten up   art

Scratched wiggly def nerves smart   art

No better connection than the word   word

With the meaning on the   side

The rap   rap

Your ears as a   guide

              Whitney Museum of American Art
                   Bowery Poetry Club

                    Jean-Michel Basquiat
                      Home on Bowery
                  His paintings verb the walls

HIT IT HITMAN! HIT IT HITMAN! HIT IT HITMAN! HIT IT HITMAN!

```
M        G                E
    E        N        P
      L  I        O        C
          T            I
            N          I
              T        F
                  O
M        G                E
    E        N        P
      L  I        O        C
          T            I
            N          I
              T        F
                    O    E
M        G            E
    E        N        P
      L  I        O        C
          T            I
            N          I
              T        F
                  O
M        G                E
    E        N        P
      L  I        O        C
          T            I
            N          I
              T        F
                  O
```

Claire Poem

(even if her birthday's day before yesterday)

Clear the air!

(The air's clear)

Clean air!

(Claire's here)

Fair Claire

       Claire's rare

          Claire dares. . . .

How doth the little crocodile

(Whoops wrong poem, that!

No crocodile roams

In Fair Claire's b-day poem

(But wouldst she not

Share said poem with croc?

I think Claire'd share it with a rock!

I know she'd share it with a shock

Of new and now and anyhow). . .)

Such flare

Voltaire

Don't swear

Prepare

No care All care

Unfair fun fair

Who dares stare

At Claire's fair hair?

No crocodilian reptilian

Gazillion cotillion

Not for a vermillion Brazilian

Couldst thou stare

At Fair Claire's hair—

Cause it's everywhere!

Because the Poem has a Life

And three and two is one tonight

For reasons that the air can't hold

As Claire herself one time me told

To get order words in order

To order not but share declare

And tear the prayer from God's own sight

On Claire's three two is one year tonight

(Or perhaps a couple days ago)

(I mean who keeps track of such trivialities?) (I dunno)

(O Claire, release us from this Poem!

It seems endless as infinite, a cloud behind the sky

Dissolves in the certainty of your eye—an eternity

Dances into a holding pattern no release

And Death is no parentheses

2 Peter Rabbit

Rabbit bows to bow of Good Ship Arrow

Dear Anne, I love you so and so NOW give big fluttery dove—

Spider Kiss to most smoocharama Hombre the Dust Planet

Has ever been trod on by

Trod on By. Trod on By.

O! dear Rabbit hoppin rock roller gravel Poet

Take me to yr ca*bin*!

Thought I saw him yesterday hiphiphoppiting the other way

O Annie, Queen! how I doth love you and him Moon Man

Rabbit Man I Do always marrying him to you

The world so different sans—I want him to complain about that

Then he knocks the golf ball into orbit

The golf ball is Earth. That's his obit.

Turning 50 at the Circus

—for Anne MacNaughton

Most Consecutive Somersaults at a Single Poetry Reading, to Anne McNaughton

For her ability to keep deep desert toes

While all about her poets, tacos

      Fax machines, land developers, pueblos,

         Chili texts, late night assignations,

            Early morning beauty blurbs, silence

               And that dove over there in the corner

Orbit and crease the Heavens with their demands

We come not to ask how you do it

We don't want to know

We come to praise the Being who does it

Sky cracks open 4 A.M.

Face of Anne

Beguiling beams

           OK you motherfuckers time to sleep!

I'm the one who stills the beast

I'm the one who sleeps the least

So slide back into your dream furrow

And write the poems for tomorrow

Patricia Spears Jones Praise Poem

2/11/01

In the Myth that is Always

Queen Patricia parks head askance gentle

Disbelief not misbelief call it full-throttle relief

Mention the highlighted detail: pink handkerchief figleaf

Fresh from Arkansas...

Should we say sass? I say sass.

Sass the sass sure can *can* the can,

And *Fresh* didn't go thisaway's *that* or thataway's *this*

Sashay! Albeit whomsoever said "Queen"

The Once and Forever Dreamer dreams

Queen Patricia Jones Spears Jones Pat where that's at

Is at! Birthday #50 a lighthouse for the crew that likes it dark

This birthday shines ordinary halo on you

All praise the day hallelu we first said Patricia

Hello to You and Welcome to the World as You Find It

Never be *that* way again! Patricia Jones been here! Walked these roads

Sang these songs wrote these poems

Made the story *become* the telephone and still

Had time for a dinner with friends that *Guidebooks to Culture*

Will ever characterize "spontaneity" their "potluck pluck and liveliness"

Patricia Dance at Own Party Jones

Patricia Friend Who Knows What Friend Is Jones

Patricia Champion Human With a Sweet Tooth and a Laugh and a Half Jones

That Makes World Its Party Jones and Patricia Celebration Jones All Praises All You Joneses!

Patricia Spears Jones!

MASSIVE PRAISE POEM
to be presented
AS INTRO FOR SHE WHO

JESSICA HAGEDORN

ASIAN AMERICAN WRITERS WORKSHOP LIFETIME ACHIEVEMENT YAHOO

While leafing through the marvelous (thanks Ken and Tsaureth!) AAWP website—can you leaf through a website, no, you must I spoze skim it but NO 'twas deeper than that, I mean look who all has piled on with the praise already for our honoree—Hong Kingston, Hwang, Shawn Wong, Kimko Hahn (even German names rhyme in Asian), Bedoya, Ish Reed, Rosal, Yamazaki and Paraiso, Zack Linmark—to be honest, all I'd have to do to get through would be to collage some of these jewel-becrusted acclamation accolades, these Kudo-laden brazen raves, decrees, degrees, gold-star feathers in her cap. I know you will read these great appreciation, approbation, citation, celebration, commendation, exaltation, laudation ovations, which so accurately take us from her early days as Kenneth Rexroth's protégée up to her reading of *Toxicology* in Sunnyside last week, not to fail to mention her diva dive at Nicky Paraiso's birthday party a week ago.

From me personally, tho, and longtime friend doesn't begin to say it, why Paloma calls me Santa Bob, Esther's disbelief from the stroller, and my dear wife all over *Toxicology,* why she's not a friend of the family, but family itself, and we all are part of hers, too. Indeed, this is a job that requires my reaching into my years of study with Papa Susso, the Gambian griot, griots being the keepers of the West African oral tradition, who are so adept at Praise Songs that they can go on for hours, just so long as the donations keep coming (yes, these are Poets who Get Paid—we can learn something from them)—Read the Damn Poem!

Hear the praises from the places and days since she was born
Waterfall of accolation

Jessica Tarahata Hagedorn

Now—

Charitable bountiful munificent & radical are not things we usually talk about without
considerable embarrassment

So I've borrowed a praise chant from the Family Dembélé of the Djibasso region of
        Burkina Faso

Ya ya the oral tradition is a way to give praise to someone without humiliating them
        totally

And now if I keep going on like this you'll probably understand why the oral
        tradition is dying

Or drop by the Bowery day after tomorrow hear Gerry Stern and Komunyakaa and
        me w/ a jazz band

Or maybe poems like this will help revive it and we'll all leave this lovely dinner
        humming this melody that

Hmmhmmhhmmhhmm

We'll be singing the praises of Jessica T Hagedorn

And I think we've now established the fact that this is gonna be a Praise Poem for
        Jessica

So I guess I'll stop singing this if you call this singing this though personally I just
        call it "Reading the Poem"

And Jessica never stopped me from reading the poem in fact she always encouraged
        me so now you can thank her

Because what I have to say melody carries meaning for

Just as Jessica's radical experimentalism in all forms of writing, in art and general is
        really just One Thing

Because the Life she lives

Is the Art she gives

Love shatters reality

Yes Jessica Hagedorn—her life is willed and wild

She keeps it simple but you can't get fancier than that

She pulls down pompous

Wrecks it with raucous

With air flagellate hair'lectric 'stonishment doesn't need hat no way

Start her in the Punk Scene, but her Beat was earlier, dig?

She came of age a poet, the last of the SF Renaissance

And Reed + Rexroth crowned her a Woman Poet—can't get better than that

She's always been the New Kid and always the Star Turn—

And the Gangster Choir
Crossed the desert and battled the Infernals

Also in 1975, Hagedorn formed a band, the West Coast Gangster Choir, rechristened in 1978 in New York City as the Gangster Choir. Earlier experiments using dramatic sketches during the pauses between songs contributed to the development of her performance art. Upon moving to the East Coast, she participated in Fay Chiang's Basement Workshop, and set foot on the Public Theater stage with Thulani Davis and Ntozake Shange—the Satin Sisters! with David Murray as band leader. Jessica says: It was a hoot! In the '80s and early '90s her performance work would continue with another triumvirate, a la the Supremes—this was Thought Music, with Laurie Carlos and Robbie McCauley.

Robbie McCauley Ntokzake Shange Thulani Davis Laurie Carlos
These women are compass points of Landscape Undiscoverable
Leading way to new understandings now taken for granted
See you at the bar
Wondering where you are
She's smoking a cigar, leans over to your ear

A poet who forges herself in a Life that burns to a crisp yet
Somehow nurtures like a tropical night
Fornicatria of the rain forest panacea, the purity of water—
Sugar & nicknames & las drogas y o Baby
"Philippines" is shorthand for Universal Blender

So when the Asian American Writers Workshop decides
Who gets Dizzying Dazzleonomy of Get Lit Bonhomie
Done up Rock Asian stylee, the Queen of the Scene will regally
Down-to-earthedly encompass all Dreams innuendoes in
Neverending gossipy syrup—pass-a de Spoon Yo!

That somehow rises like bread to make sure yr fed sprout pout
Lips sweat it out, that's Jessica literature

You will then know that words like Lifetime Achievement
Be snorted out with a retort of without a doubt—
"I Ain't Even Dead Yet"

That's when the skin peels back deliciously slowly
Revealing new baby Jessica burn churn language to lumpias
Danger and beauty Charlie Chan's booty
What'd Thought Music think of y'alls Truman Capooti?

From a review of *Pet Food and Tropical Apparitions*: A starlet recounts the sordid
sequence of her newest skin flick in which a virtuoso pianist plays "Moonlight
Sonata" while she performs sex with an anteater and five West Indians on top of a
grand piano.

And as Sam Cooke always says
But she was too young to fall in love
And I was too young to know
And if you ever change yr mind about leavin—leavin me behind
Workin on the chain gang all day long you hear them now goin
Cupid! Draw back yuh bow and let thy arrow go straight to my lovers' heart from me

Babae at Lalaki salamat sa inyo
This is the thrilling conclusion of the official formal program where Jessica
Hagedorn's laudations beyond her protestations shall depart, the Award becomes
official, and we can all sit back and eat sweets aight?

But Life will go on, and poetry will, and the Asian American Writers Workshop aka
Dizzying Dazzleonomy of Get Lit Bonhomie
Done up Rock Asian stylee, the Queen of the Scene will go on, and even after she's
Achieved a lifetime of achievement lifetime, so I guess, our dear sweet
Mother of Us All,
          Lover of All,
                    Goddess of all,
          Jessica Hagedorn she too,

Like the grand survivors of *Dogeaters, Gangster of Love, Dream Jungle,* and *Toxicology*
will go on. But tonight we

Get to just stop the river for a sec, and thank her for her gifts that

Flow like rain on this scorched earth, for the simple gift of EVERYTHING

Where art is life and life is art and thought is music

And we get to salamat her in every direction.

& now w/o further a-don't, I give the present back to she who

I give you AWWP's Lifetime Achievement Award-winner, Queen of the Scene—
Dame Babe Jessica Tarahata Hagedorn!

One Letter Poem
—Praise Poem Ide Hintze Living Alphabet

It is the letter IT{ide} which is eye 2

It is Ide my soul pal imp

Limp lamp lime times q + x + [lump] x

Ide leaps on leprechaun

Stings + bee + back

= balm honey = vinegar bend

O! olde schlag Wein RESOLVED: ¿solve?

River Tear of O   O of Tear River

And it flooooooooooows slooooooooooooooooooooooooow ne'er stoooooooooooops

v-v-v-v-v-v-v-v-v-v-v-V-V-V-V-V-V-V-V-V-∏-∏-∏-∏-∏-v-v-v-v-v-vv-v-v-v-v

Tear Wilt Palaver Go Yellow Skin Voice TearWiltPalaverGoYellowSkinVoice

Walking across street is now a Poem

Translate Celtic graffiti from The Way Back Then When

NOW READ THIS

¡¡¡¡¡*Crossing J of make that a red J and now a bounced!!!!!*

Swoosh of remembrance

Swimming cap keep

Z–z–z–nnnnn(l)

Water ears

Who hears

Coffee all

Dichter time

Perhaps human speech is animal talk body brain (?) qqqq,qqq,qq,q

And when mind enters ha t:::: bird quite proud song gfgfgf

Many more syllables alternate ll and LL depending/note (Welsh lateral "L")

Where absence lowers flower deeper growing deeper flower

Roots ah! tendrils up reaching wet Wet WET (*CRESCENDO* motherfucker!)

Blossom pushing deeperning your lovers' face oszkw

Occupying sex of river automatic payments unforseeable y–y

As the organ gets ground—where monkey at? pcdhf

Cross legs alphaalpha umlaut t–t–t–t–t–t–t–t sucher traum

And now first nut BOING a body poitreeeee sails (nailzzzzzz)

Far criss canal +++ deposits [EAR] whole gesprachen I'm-a talkin

NOT WHAT IS OBVIOUS

Coreburpbanalityslurp

Goodness, Idea! Dance, dervish! Dance!!

Wax the spot!   Ide wheels round

I am in it

Ide wheel Ide Lala Ide instrumental break Ide disincorporate

IdeIdeIdeIdeIdeIdeIdeIdeIdeIdeIdeIdeIdeIdeIdeIdeIdeIdeIdeIdeIdeIdeIdeIdeIde

what's the ide A?

! !

! !

! !

! !

! !

! !

! !

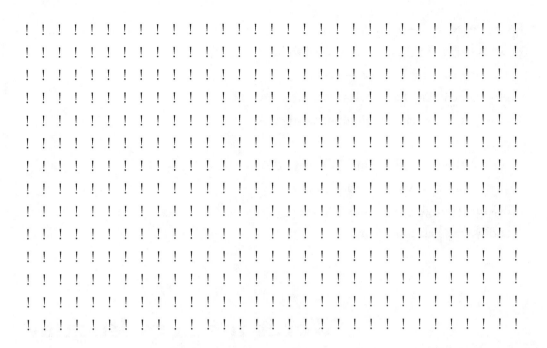

Salmon Blues
—for Bob Carroll (1942–1988)

Try out a silence from a Big Mouth Boy
Hush up the quiet in the void
Take a giant step back from the Sleepwalker's kiss
Do a laughing somersault into the abyss

Sail on, Salmon—Hoist your fins!
Nothing will start as soon as Nothing ends
Look to the sky to see the bottom of the sea
The world is a-shakin'—Volcano's gonna sneeze
That's the earth a-quakin'—it's got allergies

It's Death that's long, Art that's quick
Take a number—it's all rhetoric
Like makin' love to a porcupine
Nothin' adds up even at the bottom line

Swim on, Salmon—now you're free
& we'll spawn on the way it's sposed to be
A nagging thought of Forget-me-nots
Western medicine, he said, leaves your insides fried
I'm only here to get well enough for suicide

Sail on, Salmon—red in blue. Whadaya do
When your body won't give up on cue
So swim on mighty Salmon swim on
Goodbye my Friend goodbye

Words for Lord Buckley
—"Hipsters, flipsters and finger-poppin' daddies: knock me your lobes"

looking for words for the ever undefine future longside ya
my partner Other Ear and the Gang under the bridge hey
where's that bridge go who gives shits she dives in slices a knife
the tiny pickle-shaped molecularities are all rumba da gumbo
I am hole hollering Mama I am saying listening and you
talk now enter space of space and what place to face your
bass amazing ace place grace on the one you love it is words
under words dartin through tooth gaps smackin cheek flaps puckerin
leech meanings blabber clabber soft cream dear ass dear sweet
ass dear nose of ass smell me these words smell up page dig infinity
of tongue graspy nasty needy bleedy and the elegant hiperama
float of a word on your throat rosebud tangerine means Ed Sullivan
wordheads bird beds cranking up wellbucket overtime the Nazz
keep your hat on somebody else's head and Frank Sinatra the gasser
loved hipsemantic marijuana conga line not all said nothing is doing
lords and ladies and cats and kitties crow court is never in session always
happening where the humor flower is people words all hail the Lord

Epithalamium for
Maria the Korean Bride and
Ram Devineni,

July 2, 2012

For the Final Chapter on the Final Day!
The Wedding To End All Weddings Hey!
We are gathered here today
Because we are not gathered anywhere else today

The site of the deed that they said could never be done
On account of they could never figure
Out how Maria's 49 others could be undone
But 'tis all in fun (not really)

This wedding for my pal Ram the Groom is #1 first and only
For Maria the Korean Bride #50 and finally time to stop counting
Her eyebrows knit an Abacus of Sorrow
And a tray full of Relish. It all

Adds up to one thing only, to which our human family can attest
Maria's and Ram's families of kin and friends. Aliens and lost ones
The humongous public family of New York,
The universal family of the bluespun globe

Today, Marriage itself takes on a New Meaning
Absolving all from the Social Contract
Except for the essence of love and art
Maria and Ram
Till Life doeth them part

The Interference of Time on Love (or, Vice Versa)

—Epithalamium for Jan and Yasuo

Stone

Marriage, says Stone, is the interference of time on love (and vice versa)

Whose insolubility is all circumstance

Is about adequate to the null notion of human influence on ocean rage catacombs

Angel

Brrrring! Angel, having heard "catacombs" not a Stone's word nor throwaway, brings

Herself to full *Hello* posture, as if in drag

Which in true spilling-of-beans-while-letting-cat-out-of-combs fashion

Intercedes nein, mein, herren, quoth Angel, her freckles prickling

> marriage is the calm eye
> of calamity's ring-a-ding alarm clock

> that only works if you set it
> for love-making which creates an ever-growing bed to take care of the manifold
> generations who inhabit this garland
> of marriage, after
> murky years as paratroops
> waltzing off this passionate couple laughing
> in front of tonight's crowd

Stone

Crowd? said Stone, what crowd?

I say of the stone, it is a stone

Crowd peels off image like an orange deepening

Then accelerating, readying for the race

Angel

A reception! comprised of an organ grinder's

Monkey's tin cup shenanigans

Swallowtails swallow that's all you get

Angel
Lifting away
Lucky Pierre-style, takes

Stone
(With Campari)
But hey, when you're a Stone, what can you do?

That leaves the honest air to recapitulate:
Epithalamium for Jan and Yasuo October 30th 2007

A Nice Little Chat with a Random Guy
—Judah Atlas Bocanegra Lang's
Bar Mitzvah Praise Poem, 16 June 2012

Scramble! Scramble scramble!
Get back to words and memories
Interview me! I've disappeared

Into my own magic trick where on the 8th Day Moses
Calls for Aron to some offerings give talks like that
Wisdom Torah Parasha Haftarah
My best friend is named Elon
Bet you didn't know that rhymes with Aron
Who is not allowed to know for eight hours
About how kosher is completely split cloven hoofs
And chew their cud knowingly
Where's my cell phone at?

Is it the eight of spades?

I'll be graduating from Clinton to Brooklyn Tech

Or maybe Bard. The Queens Bard

That's what I am, the Queen's Bard!

Basketball. I used to be with a team but I hated my coach

Don't know if I'll try out for the team

But I'll try out if I like the coach

I don't like teams I like recreational. We play

On 4th Street next to the school

Language Arts that's my favorite

Reading and Writing. I hate writing but I love reading

Miss Boyd, she's a great teacher. She gives experience points

I have 20,000 experience points so I'm a sergeant major on my way

To a Jedi padawan

There's one girl, Julia Fisher, she's like a Jedi knight.

But its easier to get a 100 on a test than beating the game!

Starcraft 2 is my favorite video game

There are 3 races: the Protoss, the Terrans, and the Zergs

The Zergs are like freaky alien things, like not that advanced

They have claws or whatever

The Protoss are aliens like on Mars, with lasers

And the Terrans are humans in the future

They have Mech suits like Transformers

And you go online and because of these races

You start off with just a supply chamber

You can play another person

It's really a hundred games in one!

The Koreans are the best although they are bad at basketball

In Korea, *Starcraft 2* is like athletics

There are 200 Grand Masters in Korea

The highest league is Gold, but now I'm Bronze because my brother plays

He brings the score down

I'll just play as random

Jabba1226 is my password but don't put that in the poem

Judah Atlas Bocanegra Lang

I have the same birthday as your daughter, Sophie

Yo, let's party!!!

Purple's my favorite color. Teal was the last color I learned

Blue and red were first

These are the SCVs. They say funny things like "Hey, whatever"

They've generated things like supply depots where they refine vespene gases

They're pretty good but they're far from higher tech units

Original units just use minerals

It's impossible to make units unless you put down barracks

What I'm going to do is since they're AIs,

I'm going to make units called Ravens

They jump up and down cliffs

I'll put them behind the enemy and when the Terrans—

Oh, Terrans can fly, I forgot to tell you that—

Well, this is a bunker, they put guys in there

And they shoot out then you upgrade to orbital command

Which gets a radar thingy and you get add-ons and special abilities

Ravens get 50 gas and 50 minerals and the Protoss are using Zealots

That's cool, look at this

Here's my orbital command, see? it's orbiting already

I've got a scanner sweep

That's the energy I'm killing him with my Reaps

Oh check this out

He's attacking me with his Morks

I wouldn't recommend that

If you don't mess up your barracks, you can kill an infinite number

Of Zealots with your Reaps

Reaps aren't so good against a lot, but terrific against Zealots

There's a skill called Placement

You put their backs to the wall and they can't be surrounded

I'm pretty good at Placement

I'm going to save my ally by attacking my other enemy

Oh yeah, baby! A massive Micro guy—

The entire army got recalled!

Back it up! Attack ability, yes!!

Gee, oh god, I didn't realize there were Protoss all around my workers

My SCV which stands for something I'm not sure what

Here's a Warp Gate. The Stalker might be finishing

Then a Reap. Oh god, they're attacking me

Run, run, buddy! I'm getting wrecked,

I should've seen that coming, it's alright

The cool thing is the guys can do that and these other guys can do this

They put things in that if you're getting whacked, you can always just flee

The economy's just not that good

I'm gonna set up my shop right on that stage

I'm going to be a rapper/President/farmer/scientist

A seamless flow, not juggling things, a magician

See I'm a rapper with high political motives

I'm the President who will have a small farm at the White House

And in my spare time I'll make scientific discoveries

Being President is my least important

Maybe I'll do it in Venice—I love the Nutella there,

And the paddle boats. No, I've never been in love

Though I heard in a poem that it feels like 100 mothlings

Fluttering on my insides

I don't believe in heaven either. I think we just die

I don't see us going into an afterlife

Happiness is just contentment, I get it

Fulfilling who you are and what you want to have

Or what you need to have. Being the baby is not fun

You see in my family, well, I can't know what Ikey and my sister

Say but it used to be that they would mess with me all the time

It stopped I think because they had too much homework

But looking back it was fun

My clothes are done by my sister

Advice for the world: Don't Change

No, I take that back

Advice for the world: Global Warming Is Real

I wrote a Slam Poem to be performed with my friend Elan

We trade lines

It goes like this:

Praise Bonnet for Sam Abrams

By the bullshit of your tie and spittled joint

I will be a poet like you, if you don't mind

When you performed as Rimbaud at the Nuyorican

I knew there was a heaven and we were living it

Still, in spite of you, things go wrong

That's the purpose, Boss, of song as lid

Tyler's in your DEA jacket, the police are at the door

Dadgummit! Rochester is snoring again, tra la

Sam Abrams, Sam Abrams, your unassuming wisdom

A course of poetry and politics that informs the Earth

J'Praise J'Poem j'for J'Jerry

Jerome Rothenberg Birthday Party
Action Poetry Event @ Kitchen, 3/31/13
"Party of the Gathering" Award from the People
at the Peoples Poetry Gathering

!!!!!!!!!!!!!!!!!!!!!!!!!!!!

O what a coincidence that we needed a party they say

It's your birthday!

We praise the hairs of yr chinny chin chin Jerry Jer Jer

Home Foam Loam Dome Jerome Jerome Jerome Jerome

You who woke up the world by gentle beetle breaths just off

The edge of page You who shook the pump till the kin flowed out
Now we ken all yr kin

Children of the Rothenberg All Praise you now To you now

Speaking of which Alcheringa New Wilderness Lorca Dada Poland And the
Game of Silence A Prophecy Khurbn Big Jewish Tongue Hawk's
Well in no particular particular

Yes! we Ethnopoetics! We Ethnopoetics today!

Schwitters Millennium yes both and all

We can say is give Jerry more birthdays

Come to praise Say Jerome Rothenberg Poet hey

He's the one one now eight two in one three

Dial his number he will hold you on hold you on hold forever

His style hello Diane

And of course Charlie the music Jerry the throat Jerry the larynx
Jerry the teeth the lips

Jerry the breath Jerry the windpiping yup the Sound sound
the Unsound sound the
Unsuspecting dittlyboom lala Dada whawha sound of the
peepiepo po it it right by you

Oh we Praise love the raise the praise the dearly beloved in every

Which all Dierewcxtion zaza strain ways Jerome Rothenberg

J'Jer J'Jer we do to you

Finally

He Who Wrote Down The Oral Tradition Without Killing It

!!!!!!!!!!!!!!!!!!!!!!!!!!!!

Jerry "Jerome" Rothenberg

David Amram Praise Poems
Birthdays #70 & #80 Party
(Knitting Factory / Bowery Poetry Club)

Back in 1957 I was a French horn and little did I know I'd end up being blown by
My Man Amram in the first-ever conjoining of poetry and jazz except of course for
Those other times when lips couldn't be stripped off frozen in the heat passion of
Connections the way the kora does it in Africa when they all Praise that Guy he's
The one the Selfless one he is so full music don't stop at all a way of seeing the way
Of his neck Fetish rattling rhythm as he walks nods nonstop words roll like a piano
Roll I mean once there was just him the Amram who he am and then there was Kerouac
Did I mention next a whole gang of 'ems humans all or at least they looked that way
On the outside on the inside another story they are we are sure like Thelonious Sphere
They are all a bunch of aliens artists Beings of Otherness donchaknow but also mention
Lord Buckley Lenny Bruce Ginsberg and Corso various other Beats and Losers sore
And otherwise winners I doubt it but givers great givers and maniacs and race car
Drivers without race cars of course but there was still this goddamn piano I mentioned
I was trying to tell you tell you about piano and poem stick to the piano it was the
Piano that was rolling the way that Amram the Manram by the Damn Dam I mean
Maybe the poem will stop long enough for David Amram to hear his own name like a rest
A space eraser between notes not leave room for but it's the way he is his outgoing ongoing way
Making it happen on a roll the collaboration of the lungs with the air get it why sure it was
Rilling down the trill and rolling down the hill with a huge pail a pail that pales by all
Comparison horizon X cannot hold Mr. Amram a message on the piano roll
The holes of the roll they are out of control and they are flying so fast that the cool
Words work overtime underdone the Land of Lingo Lango where you once begun
Upon an Amram where the Praise Poem solidifies so you can wear it 'round your neck
And the musician gives birth to the poet no it's the other way 'round they were green
And they were blue and they were sort of cannot tell what hue because it seems so
Dark where they live and they got the light that goes on from the inside and the music
Did I mention it was a song they were playing but it was the words that were the
Melody and the story they were telling it was a story without words a story that makes
Itself up as it rolls everybody push it everybody roll the piano down to the man at the
Bottom who is that man at the bottom of the hill yak-yakking could it be it couldn't be it
Is the leading figure of this Praise Poem—Amram David Mr.!—and suddenly piano
Crashes into a million notes' symphonies compose as he dances them into place and
He's singing gravel and snort barks no he's listening that is us we're singing song

Praise praises Amram love gift praise more birthdays to give it all Amramwise all
Praise to sound of music the taste of the feel sight smell of music that makes itself up
Walking music the piano rolling rocks but not to sleep rock me to wake the rock the
All together now birthday clock never was before the French horn tasted lip and what
We can say is poem all that is the name the sound luscious musicality the life song of
David Amram which is name of rolling piano poet bard of musical art David Amram

All Praise Poem David Amram Birthday Numero Seventy 11/12/00 Knitting Factory y
Numero Eighty exactly ten years later you can count em on your Fingers and toes and lips
and penii ears nose throats at the Bowery Poetry Club—Baby! Which is
JUST fuckin awesome! 11/12/10

For Jack Micheline

Jack rides last train to Orinda

Sweet sleep, free fare, ne'er surrender

The artful codger, origibeat

Pure poet, soulful, now complete

Praise Ed Sanders Poem

Take stock if you would stock knock kock who's there rock

It's the Ed Sanders Praise Poem!

Spirit of Woodstock

     Noli in Spiritu Combieri

          Subscribe to the *Journal of the Center of Time*

Before the Beginning of time. . . .

Hear now the praises of places and dayses amazes scholarship hoot'n'hollership

     The Last Renaissance Man

Mark it this name chant on a pause the shifting of asses in chairs

Memories corny Kumbaya campfires/tight tomorrow's poems to be writ today

It's like Ed that day at the Olson Conference when he was seeding the future in a
       rush to begin a tradition

Someone's craning in the creek right now

Someone's spirit blowing blue out the window

Death don't stop here, a tree blossoms one

By one each place you lived

You shovel out the Mountainside as the Big One

Sun One rips the top of your head open

No it's gentle like can opener

Peer inside slightly balding pate

Never looked so sweet as the moment

When history became verse in his hand

Writ free of the Twentieth Century

Of dear Allen the Life and Times the warbling of the Fugs

How sweet he roams to his Slum Goddess Miriam the deer as equals

And all language is poem the pulsing of lyre and stupid stupid stupid heart

What a marvelous idea! to celebrate verse!

With a three-day Festival in physically beautiful place Woodstock, New York!

Festivals of course are among the most ancient of human activities

And they chanted poetry at the ancient Greek festivals, including the Olympics

Modern poetry is more free than it has ever been

In world history. Such diversity! Thank you, Ed.

Open verse, Rhymed verse, Chanted verse, Spoken verse,

Performance verse, Musical verse, Religious verse,

Erotic verse, Mad sonnets, Sane sonnets,

Even sonnets that aren't even sonnets!

If you want to write tiny rhymed couplets

On the back of postage stamps,

It's okay!

Hear em at Woodstock's best performance zones:

F-Stop Cafe Center for Photography, Upstairs at Joshua's, the astounding sounding Maverick Concert Hall, Woodstock's graceful Town Hall, the Woodstock Youth Center, the Woodstock Library, and even at the peaceful Woodstock Artists' Cemetery. *(There was an overnight Poetry Encampment last night at the nearby Opus 40 Sculpture Park. Every body who was there was there!)* Woodstock Playhouse (currently being restored), Byrdcliffe Theater, Legends of Woodstock (with its virtual museum of the Fletcher and the Hawthorne). My advice to everybody is to come hang out at the Festival, August 24–25–26, and experience some of the eternal delight that shines forth from the energy of poetry. Also organic food supply, safe air, nonpolluted water, a total end to poverty, national health care, unlimited personal freedom and fun.

So in the interest of public tranquility, we list the following places in Woodstock for visitors not to smoke pot:

1) The Artists Cemetery

2) Parking lot behind Houst's Hardware

3) Anywhere near the nightclub called the Joyous Lake

4) In the beautiful open space near the Woodstock Town Offices on Comeau Drive

5) In the Woodstock Green

6) "Down by the old Mill Stream," a swimming hole after which the famous song was named

7) The parking lot in back of the Chamber of Commerce information building

Now, on to comparing the handwriting of the rival Karmapas

Wherest puttest thou 800 pound elk on Rt 28?

Rise Up and Abandon the Creeping Meatball! (1968.2)

Dateline: 9/9/97

Woodstock is home to Ed Sanders, a poet who has inspired me, over the years, to write, to read, to redefine the job of poet to be, simply, a job. To be bard. To search out and gain knowledge, be serious about maintaining it, and pass it on. To hold on to the rigor and the vigor. To invent the new lyre. To set poetry free to be the news: to investigate. Ed Sanders is the poet/scholar/creator of Investigative Poetics.

And now, with the deaths of Ginsberg, Burroughs, Huncke, I open up the pages of the new Sanders book of poetry, *1968: A History in Verse*, full of Olson's open form, Ed's Egyptian glyphs, footnotes, jokes, photos, ephemera. In *1968* rock and politics shared the air, and Ed's playful, incisive language serves as time machine: if you were there (*1968* as Place), it will cause you to resurrect that other world; if you weren't, you'll never believe that that year was squeezed into a year.

Ed Sanders and his Magic Pulse Lyre

Ed Sanders, lead warbler of the Fugs

Ed Sanders editor of *Fuck You: A Magazine of the Arts*

Ed Sanders currently editor of his own weekly, *The Woodstock Journal*

Of Ed Sanders, we ask, "What does the poet say in times like this? What do we
      sing?"

"We demand the Politics of Ecstasy!"
      our leaflets thunder

"Rise Up and Abandon the Creeping Meatball!"

"—though, 30 years later, it seems a tactical error

to announce that 500,000 people

      were going to make love

         in Chicago parks." [p.17]

"I don't care what you sing,

but if you jack off that microphone

      one more time

I'm going to arrest you." [p.23]

"Nothing overt occurred

   no hover-job, no mist, no noise, no clank, no rustle."

      [during Exorcism of Sen. Joe McCarthy's gravesite, p.25]

Drawing the Line: Ed Sanders' *1968* is Poetry Book of the Year

Dateline: 8/26/97

My wife is an artist. I'm a poet. She draws, I end lines. This summer of '97 we lie in bed in early morning upstate New York and watch trees come to light. We drink coffee in bed, we read, we talk. Elizabeth is reading *Middlemarch*, and gasps amazed with the smarts of a writing circling the Reader until Reader is inside, is all the characters. The world vibrates. I am reading Ed Sanders' investigative poetics text

1968, the most amazing year of the century seen afresh and personal as Ed leads the Fugs through the year of Chicago and RFK assassination. Occasionally we will chortle or cry in surprise, and bring the Other up to date.

Mayor Daley's people did not take kindly to Abbie Hoffman's smoking pot in the Mayor's chambers. I chortle. The image cracks me up: "Right On!" to Abbie's refusal to bend to hypocrisy. I read the section to E. "This is why the '60s failed," she starts in. "Little boys playing their games, getting even with Mommy and Daddy." Wonderful passion—yes, the participants were all white middle class men. The Yippie movement was so infiltrated by cops—1 in 6 at Chicago park demonstration were undercover. Daley had no plans to grant permits, anyway. The Motherfuckers and Chicago radicals were opposed to the demo sans permits.

Do you get a permit to have a revolution?

What did we know? Nothing.

Say he had granted a permit—then it would have been "Stand over here in lines in a part of the City where no one would notice." Hoffman began things on an even footing—"your halls of power, my cultural mores." I may not be good at analysis, and pot may not be an issue to kill over, but freedom is what Yippies were all about. Let Daley have his martinis. Smoke the pipe, as the Natives do.

By now E is back in *Middlemarch*. And I am reading about Terry Southern and William Burroughs joining with Ed and Allen in Chicago, hours of Om to keep the calm calm.

This is 1997, not the most amazing year of the century, but Year of Death in the Beat Generation—Huncke, Ginsberg, Burroughs. But we have He Who Refuses to be Burnt Out, torch-bearer Ed Sanders, providing us with Way Forward Through the Past.

1968 by Ed Sanders is Poetry Book of the Year.

> Like the Captain in Star Trek says, "We don't know now, but maybe
> we'll find it out in the past."
> "From now on, nothing holds us back. Cacaphony forever. No stopping."
> —*Ed Sanders, at the first Fugs recording session*

> "The Fugs are not Rock'n'Roll Hall of Fame residents
> Nor staples on VH-1 and are to be admired for it."
> —*Hymn to the Rebel Café*

Frenzy, Wet Dream and Ramses II Is Dead, My Love.

Miriam

Now I see I have taken time and not gone anywhere which is the purpose of a
    Praise Song to lead us right here
When here is Woodstock the Festival zap coordinates this stage this mic this
    mouth these words for Ed Sanders our Bard
So without and with ado and adon't and a will a way the man who gives us
    everything and we don't mind accepting it
This is the fulfillment of the vision of the poem of the Mongolian cluster fuck as
    translated to a full mental jacket

Praise Ed Sanders Poem

My Man Lev

You postered the university with handouts stating there would be a poetry reading
You have no idea how long I had been looking at that wall waiting for that poster
    to appear
And I was early at Forlini's Third Phase but I of course would not buy anything
    "Where is the poetry reading"
Downstairs is the poetry reading. Way down there
In the pawpaw patch
My poems came fast then
They wrote themselves about feet and girls and boys and rocket ships and dogs
I heard you read so easy, so effortlessly. I wanted to write like you
So I wrote for you and things fell into place
Now you come to my place and we share a beer, it's sweet the way the poetry
Rolls like long hair over such big ears we have
So much poetry the world stands at attention
We'll sit at ease
Life's a breeze
Don Lev's word is "Hyn"

The way you gave it to Fidel Castro and *Putney Swope* on the street corner Harlem
Hynglorious! Hynalicious!
Hyn!

A Little Something
—for Enid Dame

Angry chefs are writing poems
The poets are making chicken soup, tasty tasty
The firemen are setting fires and the firewomen are firing the firemen
"If that's your job you don't have job no more!"
The Cedars of Tavernon are busy swaying and shading the gravesite
And the rocks are growing
So quickly the only job is filing down their fingernails
With electric drills and cheese graters (you get to wear headphones)
Luckily homeless people want to read my poems
I stand at the newsstand making mouth moves "I can't stand it!" noiselessly
Maybe all I'm saying is it's a real job, being unemployed

It's not on TV
Not even on the radio
It's not in *Books in Print* or *Out of Print* or *Digital Books Could Care Less for Print*
You cannot skywrite it from a bipolarplane, spray paint on a dijiririgible
Your mother rocked you to sleep with it, that's all
And you didn't even know it because you fell asleep and the words sailed clouds
In starry water over blue sandcastled grassy grassy hills

Animals can talk, they are movie stars
And war. War is forgotten. What was war? says the pug to the poodle
As they nosh on a noodle pudding
Served by Enid Dame who has a real job
Cue Lillith, the banjo cantor,
A job here on earth, no tips allowed
Enid, this chicken soup is for you
To give away, too

Frank Robinson

Oh racist Cincinnati!
Crosley Field with Robby in left!
Elegant impassive burning
Here's the five who hit more homers:
Aaron, Bonds, Ruth, Mays, Sosa.
That's It List, Hit List!
(Update: Steroid Crush News, now he's #10)

Racism and Free Agency

So Curt Flood played right those first two years

(Frank: Rookie of Year 1956)

But Cincinnati couldn't handle so many blacks on team.

Flood is told no raise because of franchise financial problems,

Speaks out, is traded to Cards—Racism At Root

Of Free Agency! Read poem all about it!

The Worst Trade Ever

Robinson to Baltimore, 1966.

Reds left behind and white to become Big Red Machine.

Pete Rose, outsider, hung with Robby and Vada Pinson.

Does Robinson's departure push Rose into bookies' arms?

Frank Robinson, first Black manager in majors, 1975.

Manager, Washington Nationals, 2002.

Robinson in Washington

Which is where he gets W's attention.

Awarded Presidential Medal of Freedom, 2005.

In photo Robinson looks presidential.

Little shuffling white guy, embarrassed recipient.

Aretha Franklin, seated behind them, knows

Who to sing "Respect" for.

Respect For

Frank Robinson, who was traded "an old 30"

Says Reds front office, translates "too many

blacks on team" to the Orioles for Milt (Who?)

Papas, 1966, same year I leave Cincy
("Porkopolis," Larry Flynt, Mapplethorpe art bust, et al)
For New York, Frank O'Hara dies, Robinson wins
Triple Crown, AL MVP (only player to win MVP
In both leagues), leads Baltimore to World Championship

Robby Approaches 2nd on a Potential Double Play
Run gunning full clock speed handle axe
Hands clawing high in air aim direct pivot man
Last possible moment fear—wait—slide
Tumbling UP (impossible!) dust to rolling body block
How's that for a finish and if he happens to be somewhere
In the vicinity of second so much the better

Hanlon Stuart Poem Praise

OPENUP!!

Hope-ope-hopen-up

Open up!

Kathy Stuart Hanlon Liam and Rory Hanlon Kamel Bob Elizabeth Sophie Daisy
Molly Peter Nita Tony Sheila George Dan Matt Harpo Joey Caitlan John and Marny
GeeGee Geronimo! Johnny Michael Bumblebee Nancy and all of the SLA NLG ACLU
    acronyms not acronimity
Columbia Hartley Tiemann Broadway Pacific Street Pennsylvania crossing Canada with
    Janis Joplin and the band in a van
Stuart Street York Street Duboce and Belvedere Streets Sea Ranch not to mention
    sidetrips Ireland Italy Greece (in hock to Morocco)
Hear the praises from the places and days of this loving lug generous man

Now

      Let's sing the praises of Stuart Douglas Hanlon

And I think we've now established the fact that this is a Praise Poem

So I guess I'll stop singing this if you call this "singing"

This though personally I just call it "Reading the Poem"

Cause Stu never stopped me from reading the poem

In fact he always encouraged me

So now you can thank him

In fact that's what makes sense of this moment

What makes us dress up and traipse cross town, cross country

Hop over from Hawaii and up from Louisiana to utilize precious Saturday evening
      in Just Spring

We have agreed on this moment to corner this guy in a room

Where the purpose No Purpose At All thanking somebody, praising him for
Friendship

Sending appreciations like flowers delivered in fogstorm

Friendship = Antipraise

Love is a dailiness

      The eye of the day

          And the you of the night

            And so we come to gather, huddle together

              Against the rages of the light

Not to stop the ongoingness

But to barely mark it to pause the clanking

Of plates, ice tinkles, circling waiters who all

Want to grow up to be cowboys (girls

Can be cowboys too) and lawyers and poets

And recently freed people we call heroes because

They are

      People if anyone wants to grow up tonight

A violin scratching across the page to praise

It is less like a garden tended with

An unremarkable glance up towards

Twin Peaks above Upper Haight

Someone's craning in a new hottub tonight

Someone's spirit is blowing blue out the window

Death don't stop here, a tree that blossoms one

By one each branch is a place

Where you live you work you hang you chill

You shoot the baskets you weave the baskets each leaf

A memory and the blossoms collect around your feet

And you shovel out the tide as the big one

The sun rips the top of your head open

No it's gentle like can opener

Peer inside slightly balding pate

Of our dear bearded host I mean I know he's not the host

The Lawyers Guild is he would never have ordered chicken

But it is his role to be centerpiece so let him

Let him as he is father of and widower of

And freed people from prison of and the bayous of

Never looked so sweet as the moment when

History stopped and let a man walk free and

When history stopped and people who would change the ineffable

Via revolutionary fervor and stupid stupid stupid heart sent to prison

Through it woven like a praise chant, to say no, I can't leave

The boys to mark the man a man—friendship

Fairness riding shotgun on unfairness and

Clarity patience generosity and like the time he gave away his car

He gave away car!

He put his head through the wall he answered the phone drawing attention to the
cribbage games and the handwriting the discipline what is it makes us human is
what he's got the swinging ashtray for the girlfriends and taxi jobs and lsd in the
ruling class cocktail soirees djellaba at Hastings

To praise him is not the deal

We are here in a place

Hold that place

Hold this time

Memory in Progress

But it's our dailiness that will hold

As ji-Jaga Geronimo 27 years in prison 8 in solitary COINTELPRO railroaded
    him there

Johnny Cochran hires him assistant Stuart Hanlon college student in djellaba

Johnny goes about his business, Stu hangs in there for the distance

End of story: Gee is finally free, FBI handed over million bucks

First time they ever paid up a pay out

You go Geronimo not stopping here no more

Africa calls. Africa is the door.

Just a little moment here

A thank you to

    A Praise Poem for Stuart D. Hanlon

             For what you do, did, and done

Freedom means not to be on the run

Not to be stuck in the goddamn cell either

Just a moment's breather, a life

Either I say it, or We're all Poets

So get up off the floor motherfuckers

Let's roar this moment into being

It's each other that we're freeing

Big Stu
This one's for you

Ode to the Lemon Ice King

We are gathered here tonight to sing
Praises to the Lemon King!

To lick the cup, life's fleeting pleasure
An absolute New York refresher treasure
How many tastes
How many smiles
How many mmmmmmmmms
Fuggidabout it—it's beyond measure

What is the appropriate
Absolutely not disproportionate approach
To the delectable
Selectable
Ineluctable
Retractable
Licking of the cup

First pinch the pleats
Twixt thumb and index
Feel the seep of cold take hold
Feel the chill thrill fill
The ooooo natural reflex
Your thumb your index
Now bring yr oh so virtuoso
Bottom lip to lip of cup
Reach your tongue around and up
And feel young feel young
Aswirl atwirl a curl of tart and sweet
Icy nicey loaded dicey
Twice thricey what's the pricey
Close your eyes, taste the zing
Royal visit to the Lemon King

So much better than ice cream
From a truck that goes ding-a-ling
And I'm not just talkin' bout the taste
Ice is better for the waist

Though his throne's a glassed-in palace
Though the crown he wears is cotton
There are some things in Lemon Kingdom
That should never be forgotten

For the King of Queens he must ordain
During his *sessanta due*
Sixty-two-ay year-reign
Ices must by eaten plain

Though the folks at the shop are the nicest
THEY WILL NOT MIX OR EXCHANGE ICES
Every nudnik bows in favor:
Ices are a single flavor
And do not ask him for a scoop
They use a shovel—not a scoop
With an ice, a cup, an alley oop
That flips the ice fantastic
Shovel's real steel never plastic
You wanna make a mess
When you could taste the pure, the best
Solomente! Solo! No in-between!
Don't mix the yellow with the green
Lemon with pistachio?
It's a big Corona no No NO
And peanut butter better batter up alone
Or stick it up your sticky cell phone

If you want to make the scene
Make it with the only King of Queens

Peter Benfaremo
If you only know what he know
No matter where you gonna go
Que bella bellaissimo
For nothing's nice as lemon ice
Served by Benfaremo

So tonight we give a token before this esteemed crowd
To the man who wears the crown
Pete Benfaremo and his incredible Persona
As the Lemon Ice King of Corona
Where Dapper Don and Don the Dork
And everyone who gets outta work
Brings their finest fancy champagne-date
To the place Corona-ites congregate
Spaghetti Park's across the street
And half the universe shows up to meet
Sweet Pete Signore Benfaremo
Pete the Lemon King
Sees puddles of sticky-fingered sunshine sizzling
On the sidewalks of New York

Trip the ice fantastic
Drip enthusiastic
Pop the cork
The Lemon King of All New York!

The Prairie
—*for James Gandolfini*

The prairie for James Gandolfini the stage for James Gandolfini the TV screen for James Gandolfini the mountain is James Gandolfini yes Jimmy's a shy monster yes he is

The General James Gandolfini is so specifically James Gandolfini he's Tony he's the Boss we call him Dad James Gandolfini

The white bathrobe of James Gandolfini walks past the pool down the driveway to get the newspaper The New York Times is James Gandolfini is wha? obituary stunned and Star-Ledger is James Gandolfini

Mercedes is James Gandolfini's preferred method of sausage James Gandolfini with the prairie of James Gandolfini making sausage Nietzsche is James Gandolfini the mind of James Gandolfini an ocean of Jim and on stage a tiger he was everyone's James Gandolfini kind of like breathing James Gandolfini kind of like praising James Gandolfini he was everyone's James Gandolfini

Bird with No Mouth
—*for Philip Seymour Hoffman*

How do you hear the Bird with No Mouth?
Inside the box that is your mind/safe/cupboard
Of gray. Solitude sparks electricity bolts, rifle
Gray matter, blown dust liquidity, luminous blank.

The Voice only speaks because in this place
Song's reduced, meme's melody separated.
You see feel taste smell words as gray
Moistening meaning, flow boiling capacitors.

What may this cannot-sing, knowing Bird say?
Meaning gray plane on hill, solid one-plank
Bridge swinging vocabulary rippling cortex
Who fits there with you, slides in beside?

The news isn't good, Bird is sorry to say.

Makes too much sense. Black beak breaks!

Someone has gone, whirled, left world behind.

Lackluster lick rhyme, gray gray with gray.

A True Account of Ntozake Shange's Luminous Appearance at the Harlem Poetry Salon Spreading Life, Love and Poetry to Everyone a Week Before She Passed

The Cast

Quincy Troupe

Margaret Porter Troupe

Victor Hernández Cruz

Willie Perdomo

Nancy Mercado

Urayoán Noel

Ed Morales

Mariposa (María Teresa Fernández)

Pedro Pietri

Edwin Torres

Lydia Cortez

The Heckler

Felipe Luciano

Umar Bin Hassan

Abiodun Oyewole

Fay Chiang

The Basement Workshop

Savannah Shange

David Murray

Amiri Baraka

Spaceman

Gwendolyn Brooks
Poetry Project at St. Marks Church
Jessica Hagedorn
Robbie McCauley
Laurie Carlos
Miguel Algarín
Héctor Lavoe
Thulani Davis
Bob Kaufman

Just one of those Harlem Sunday afternoon salons at Quincy and Margaret's where
the starting time is 2 p.m. and when you get there at 3 you're early

        It's Victor's day, PR Day,
Borinquín, *Beneath the Spanish* he lyricizes, canonizes
the debonair air, the melodious flow

        Taino, bomba y plena, emergent
Morocco, life in the shadow of *español*

                Been there
                Being there
                Always there
                Home in Harlem

Where Willie opens the barrio, that corner where it all begins.
Nancy Supermarket, joy and anger intermixed,
Global Warming burning mad sing flinging, we're all an ear here where
Urayoán gets the university woke, the Academy of Cheverechevere,
articulate matriculate, tossing robes and mortars
while chairing the high session Latinx 101 is Prof Ed, poet-of-
back-in-the-day, visionary journalist *el jefe aché*. Who else but
Mariposa and the liftoff voice of truality, flying, hello! Pedro's
hovering in the wings. Nuyofuturismo in la casa,
Edwin rising up and over and into into, locus: hocus focus.
Lydia o Lydia grounds poetry's history her story, the crowd
percusses, happening maracas, back to you, Victor, *soavacito siempre*

In *otras palabras,*
Home. Harlem. 'Til all is said and almost done which is *el momento cuando*
Felipe shows, allowing Heckler's triumph, "Now you see
why they're called *The Last Poets!*" Indeed.
Launching into Young Lords *politipo,*
call forth the last Last Poets, Umar, Abiodun

> Trip flip
> Race space
> Time place

Q's *Voice* article from back in that day
changing everything into today
Esta misma casita de bienvenidos
Harlem ReRenaissance
Cue food *delicioso y perfecto* when
a buzz in a corner combusts a tsunami to drown in

She Appears

Zake walks in Queen resplendent
Zake appears all lights shimmer down glow
Zake's in the house, forks clatter floor
Zake's here now, Last Poets ain't last anymore

Zake sidles up, whispers into Margaret's ear,
We all aflutter to overhear
Then in laughter, Margaret lets it be known
There will be no nicotine for this woman on the throne!
Instead, Open the window on 7th Avenue!
Jump, Zake, jump! I'll not enable
your death by cigarette, sister Paulette,
all you been through. . . .

And a week later she will pass.

The doctor's daughter, holding court in Fay's basement,
that poem about her daughter, Savannah. Laughing over that
with David in Paris, before his sax rollicked the everlast, Amiri there.
Over to Spaceman, her guitarist, laying down the sound bed
gravel her voice formed poems from, coming

And that time at the church with Gwen, handing off poetry's baton,
"Read the *poem* Poems!" and she did

        Jessica, Robbie, Laurie,
they *Thought Music*. Zake pushes, presides, tradition carrying, unburying

        The ashtray she threw at Miguel spins into orbit, waltzing
on the Princeton stage, the Marriage of *la Poesía y el Teatro*

Oh shit. It's snowing in the poem, *ridiculoso*
Each flake a different shape poem
Zake. Ntozake "Change!" Shange
Parade route of paper, make that "poem confetti"
Sung by Hector to open for Thulani
Who responds to Times obit "a performer turned playwright"
Whaaa??? All praise all things Zake, Queen of Poetry
The Choreopoem that Went All the Way to Broadway
How poetry changes lives she lives
All praise our dear Sister Zake
The punch of kiss that will not miss
Word after word that must be heard
For Colored Girls Who Have Considered Suicide
When the Rainbow is Enuf, Bob tells me
You can't put rainbows in your poems anymore
'Cept for Zake

'Cept for Zake

All Praise Ntozake Shange Praise All

Last Line of
Ellen Stewart's Obituary

She left hundreds of thousands
Of immediate survivors.
Do not wear green to the funeral.

Sowing Stars

—for Helen Tworkov

This much I can tell you
There is nothing easy about ease
There's nothing difficult about difficulty
Eagle's claw unclenches and the egg
     begins slo-mo descent
That is birth hurtling inevitable and the wind
Blossoming selfless concern, blue spruce and spume

Say you are atop a unicycle and the population of the world
Is lined-up single file on your shoulders
Balancing, prepping, to pass through into The Future
Which is not to be seen and of which I can tell you nothing
Except this: one day you call it the Gulf Stream
     of Contentment and the next
It's the Undertow of Desperation
You can go from zero to seventy in 3.9 seconds
     and if there's a brick wall it's still kiss
     the airbag if you're lucky
So as we wait on line, the Now bicycle to the future
Breaks down giving good excuse for everybody to party party
It's our tricycle, and we can party if we want to
All Praise to Helen, for all she gives is Everything!
This Poem of Praise Helen Tworkov, from the Lookout
On the tilted edge of Sight Cove
Amidst the awesome resound of Cape Breton
Isle Margaree, single eye reflecting single star
Solitude of the multitude, New York amidst all this night
Song and poem, living grace,

       Praise Helen, Friends, embrace!

All Praise Cecil Taylor

"Rhythm is the Life of Space of Time danced through."
—Cecil Taylor

Them laugh them cry them fingers flip wise
Troll the riverbed dead not dead not dead
Once after the concert you told me it was not after the concert
This is the concert is just what you said
I remember that now along with dead not dead not dead
So a blew note blows trill still the hurricane of silence
You mentioned how the string got unstrung and when it rung
That's where it begun so begin again a little closer to the end
Where the bend won't bend and the bang hangs a blend
Right at the point and left with the joint just hammer
Hammer the pale night nail (hammer the pale night nail)
The jawdropper corral where the pedal dance flail
That's the cozy up to it reborn, where the Stop sign is a square
Baby understands, rocks the baby grand and rolls the key
Till the lock screams "I Give" and all the dough
Comes rolling up to Heaven's creak, squeak squeak

Altogether Call Together!

A People's Poetry Gathering Genesis Lift-Off
for the United Sates Department of Arts and Culture

IN THE BEGINNING
there was the poem
and the poem was made of words
and the words were made of letters and sounds
and the letters and sounds were made by people
and so the people had these poems made out of words

of letters and sounds all over the world so the people gathered

the poems together and it was

IN THE BEGINNING

and it *was* The Beginning: Altogether Call Together

for the People's Poetry Gathering, a long-division non-divisive component

of the aptly named

United States Department of Arts and Culture

a living anthology

a cabinet seat where the cabinet is filled with breathing art

and not cut-glass gravy boats

and Stanley Kunitz says it's a populist bacchanal and

Jerry Rothenberg calls it a Woodstock of Poets and

the poems are strung on clotheslines provided by the cordel poets of Brazil

and written by cameras for Berlin's Zebra Poetry Film Festival

and the poems are played

on the 21 strings of the kora

provided by Papa Susso

and all other griots of West Africa

and the poems are four-hour long solo operas provided by the P'ansori poets
of Korea and are Yoiked by the Saami poets above the Arctic Circle and the
philosophical philological semiotical deconstructivistarooni poets argue long
into the night about the Meaning of Meaning and whether the Gathering is
a gathering of po*ETS* or po*EMS*, until Gregory Corso sits up from his coffin
and howls: "Make the Poet's Choice! Take both of 'em!" and the Dub poets
proclaim Bass Culture and the Eritrean poets proclaim poetry in nine languages
spoken in one country of 3.5 million and the cowboy poets ride in

on the range which is arranged in rhyme royale

as invented by Chaucer

who is also gathered here today as is Emily Dickinson

and Walt Whitman, Gwendolyn Brooks, Frank O'Hara

and Amiri Baraka, Ginsberg and Neruda, Wanda Coleman,

Pedro Pietri, Sekou Sundiata and Muriel Rukeyser and June Jordan and Li Po and
Tu Fu and Federico Garcia Lorca all of whom are simultaneously

at the International Poetry Festival

in Medellín partying with Fernando Rendón

and the Slam poets all get tens and Youth Speaks for itself because they're all poets

and the hiphop poets go on y on

'til the break of dawn

and the Appropriationist poets have already claimed this poem
is their poem and the concrete poets have shaped this poem
into the shape of an ever-growing universe poem
complete with a Higg's boson even
and the Basque poets are *bertsolariaking* with the Jazz poets
improvising with the Tuvan poets who are throat-singing and
the Endangered Language Alliance is sponsoring
the Breton-Garifuna Poetry Dance Party
and the Trinidadians are doin' extempo mon and the decimistas
are counting to diez in Borinqua as the loggers log on
and the fishermen poets hook us
and the taxi poets proclaim themselves Hack Poets
and the poets who eschew any name for themselves
but the word *poet* even they allow as how they can gather
when the purpose of gathering is poetry
for the people *of* the people *by* the people
and the words themselves order themselves to be made
of the letters of the sounds all of which are actually people
and when we get that far when people are not only the po*ETS*
but are also the po*EMS*
then the Peoples Poetry Gathering becomes this
Altogether Call Together
under the elephant umbrella of the
United States Department of Arts and Culture
where words manifest as poetry, never having to ask
or answer the question: Is that a Real Poem
or did you just make it up yourself?
because as Dr. Willie used to say, we are Gathered here today because we're not
gathered anywhere else today
and we're all poets anyway
all nations, under art, divisible to each heart
united in single poem
that reads itself to you to put yourself to sleep
in the good night of billions of stars where you dream the poem never even
imagining that you will have to wake up
because you already are awake and working
a real job writing poems, dancing, making paintings and movies

and sculpting and singing
which is where the poem stops
with the words
IN THE BEGINNING
and
IN THE END

This Is It!

The World is ending! &
The piano is playing &
The artwork is
All of us on stage!

Lift your voices & lift
The roof & lift the sky
& Heavens & fr chrissakes
Sing!

This Is It!

Notes

Prelude

Hey You and **By The Book** *(p. 1)* The last words of my notes for *The Collect Call of the Wild* were Theoreau's: "My life is the book I would have writ/ but I could not both live and utter it." That book came out twenty-some years ago and I've written extensively since then, publishing two collections but so busy have I been living my life and uttering the poems that it takes this book to bring us up to date. Originally called *Bob Holman and the Spoken Word Movement,* Cathy Bowman suggested *(A Book [Not A Performance])* as a subtitle, all the better to drive home the orality-text conundra. I love books, don't get me wrong! It's just that it's awfully quiet in here. So anyway, until you hear these words, let this book exist in the folds of the Special Place where reading creates reality. In other words, *The Unspoken Word* that only you can hear. (Big shoutout to Cathy, deep reader of this book. Also, Paolo Javier for *SPOKUN,* an alternate universe.)

Because I always say, "There's no such thing as a performance poem," I had to write **Performance Poem.** *(p. 1)* When I perform it, I sometimes follow the directions of the text, diving off the front of the stage during the first line, beckoning the tech crew to follow my instructions as I run through the crowd. Usually I get the audience into the act, especially the keening part ("You know, like at a wake"). At the World Heavyweight Poetry Bout in Taos (shouts to Annie MacNaughton and dear departed Peter Rabbit), where my opponent was Sherman Alexie, I leapt from the ring and took the wireless mic out into the parking lot, still doing the poem, which just goes to show you: Never take on Sherman Alexie in Native Country. Other times I simply read the poem straight, let the audience imagine. Imagine that!

The Death of Poetry *(p. 3)* can be found on *In With the Out Crowd* (Mouth Almighty/Mercury Records), produced by Hal Willner.

Letter to Elizabeth *(p. 11)* I don't know how Elizabeth got into the "Prelude" section, except it seems she's in every section. **I Thought** *(p. 12)* is a linked poem to **Letter.**

Night Day

The Poem *(p. 15)* was commissioned by Satellite Collective for their Telephone artpiece, an ekphrastic collaboration that included 315 artists by its conclusion. I was in on Nathan Langton's concept from the start, which was the Breton Sailor's prayer beginning, "Oh God, Thy Sea Is So Great and My Boat is So Small," which inspired a painting by Jana Weaver. Jana's painting in turn inspired this poem. And so on, to 315 iterations. (*See* http://telephone.satellitecollective.org)

Bob Holman's 343rd Dream *(p. 16)* All dreams guaranteed real.

Disappearing Into Vision *(p. 16)* Ayahuasca. When I confronted Cecilia Vicuña about her appearance in my dreamquest, she recounted the tale where the shaman was unwilling to give her the Medicine. Understood.

Good Questions (DREAM) is a birthday poem. I write one a year, and often for others as well, see also **Dear Elizabeth Hello** *(p. 28)*, **Without You** *(p. 20)*, **No Allusions to Closeness of Closeness I Pray** *(p. 27)*, **You Can Have My Husband (But Please Don't Mess with My Man)** *(p. 33)*, **You Are the Corner of My Eye** *(p. 41)*, **Rocket Birth Day** *(p. 48)*, **STEP** *(p. 67)*, **A Real Stage and Like a Punk Festival or Something Cool and Loud Salsa** *(p. 88)*, **J'Praise J'Poem, for J'Jerry** *(p. 158)*, **David Amram Praise Poem**. *(p. 159)*

Another Poem *(p. 18)* I played the title role in the Yara Arts production of *Captain John Smith Goes to Ukraine* in 2013/14, in Kiev, Lviv and at LaMama, NYC. Thanks to Virlana Tkacz, Julian Kytasty, Susan Hwang. This poem plays with the oral epic idea of spontaneous composition exemplified by Ukrainian Kobzars, blind bards, and their epics, *dumy.*

Potato *(p. 18)* was written for and published by *Spud Songs: An Anthology of Potato Poems: To Benefit Hunger Relief* (1999, Helicon Nine Editions), Gloria Vando and Robert Stewart, Editors.

Later for Now *(p. 23)* also appears on *In With The Out Crowd,* a duet with Chris Spedding on guitar.

Movements

The Opening of the Big Museum *(p. 32)* for the presto change-o at MoMA, 2004

You Can Have My Husband (But Please Don't Mess with My Man) This Praise Poem (also a Birthday poem! [well, a half-birthday]) is the one that Chuck Close heard that inspired our collaboration, *A Couple Ways of Doing Something.*

Impressions, *(p. 34)* inspired by a show at the Clark in Williamstown, an ekphrastic series, joining such as *The Cutouts (Matisse)* (PeKa Boo Press, 2017), "Van Gogh's Violin," "Rothkos," "Immediately Poems" (in *Sing This One Back To Me*, Coffee House, 2013), *Picasso in Barcelona* (Paper Kite, 2011), *A Couple Ways of Doing Something* (collabration with Chuck Close, Aperture, 2006), and *Talking Pictures*, Kristi Zea's film based on my poems inspired by Elizabeth Murray paintings (double ekphrastic!), 2019. Here the poems are the paintings, I suppose, but they also suggest that the painter Get back to work! The painter wishes the poet to do the same.

Something Allen Once Gave Me *(p. 49)* Ginsberg, of course.

To Pringleize *(p. 49)* is a neologism I coined for the "No Chains on Bowery" division of the "Stop 7-Eleven" campaign to save the neighborhood's bodegas.

Dance

Stravinsky's "Three Pieces for Clarinet Solo, III." *(p. 51)* Composed by and performed with Michael Drapkin. Includes postcard designed and printed by Purgatory Pie Press. Shoutouts to Esther K. Smith and Dikko Faust.

Dancing w/ Destiny *(p. 53)* For Timbila: Nora Balaban, Banning Eyre, Rima Fand, Louisa Bradshaw, Dirck Westervelt, Bill Ruyle. I've written numerous lyrics for this African-influenced band over the years, and couldn't be happier. They made a video of this one, up on YouTube.

Double Beginning *(p. 55)*, **STEP** Many thanks to Molissa Fenley. These poems appear in her book, *Found Object*. **Double Beginning** was performed at the 92nd St Y, **STEP** *(p. 67)* was created at the Atlantic Center for the Arts in 2008 and performed at Judson Church 2009 https://www.youtube.com/watch?v=4PJj7EBkNdY. My standard method of collaborating with dance is to go to rehearsal, translate gesture to imagery to language, rehearse. If everything is in order, perform with dancers on stage.

For Everybody in the World Dancing *(p. 74)* Commissioned and performed with Sarah Skaggs and Dancers in Bryant Park, 1999.

Ornettes Jeffrey Sichel had the idea to turn Umberto Eco's *Island of the Day Before* into an opera. I was doing the libretto and Ornette Coleman was doing the music. We made a couple of visits to Ornette's studio/loft and I was able to glean these poems toward the production before the dream fabric wore through (or was it the budget?). Originally published in *Jacket 2*.

Home on the Road

Papa Was a Peddler *(p. 81)* Solomon and Sophie Geller left the village of Kamianets-Podilskyi, Ukraine and somehow landed in Harlan, Kentucky, where my father, Benjamin Franklin Geller, was born.

The Village *(p. 82)* When I host the Greenwich Village Society for Historic Preservation Villager Awards, this poem is the invocation. Published in their book, *Village Stories*.

Inside the Synagogue is Mars *(p. 84)* Abe Orensanz's favorite poem, this was read at his memorial.

On Mars *(p. 86)* Hal Sirowitz and Minter Krotzer and Bijou the Poodle.

14th Street *(p. 86)* Commissioned for the 14th St show, Art in Odd Places.

Rain *(p. 90)* Danny O'Neil tapped me to work on "Poetry Spots" for WNYC-TV in 1984. He died of AIDS before our first season. For Roberto Bedoya.

Nickname *(p. 90)* Big joke in the bar business is *to use a bar as a dropoff spot*, taking me back to my college job as a singing bartender at Your Fathers Mustache Banjo Bar, where I once left a first edition of a Shaw play for Eric Bentley. Learned my lesson.

Occupy *(p. 91)* Appeared first in the giant Occupy Wall Street poetry anthology, compiled by Stephen Boyer and Filip Marinovich.

US Poet Delegation Kolkata Book Fair 2008 *(p. 92)* Commissioned by Gary Gautam Datta. Others in the Delegation: Ram Devineni, Catherine Fletcher, Carolyn Forché, Nathalie Handal, Joy Harjo, Erica Jong, Yusef Komunyakaa, Christopher Merill, Dante Micheaux, Idra Novey, Ed Pavlić, Paul Theroux.

Charlie Listens *(p. 95)* Charlie Mangulda, last speaker of Amurdak, had sung his Spirit Language songs thousands of times, but the first time it was recorded was a different story. In Amurdak, there is neither left nor right; cardinal directions suffice. One of the few instances where the consciousness of a language can be scientifically adjudicated. It was during this re-recording session that Charlie allowed he knew a few words in Wurridik, a language heretofore thought extinct. Sometimes the cameras do create a moment. Deep bows to Charlie Mangulda, Jamesy Mang-Ida, Nick Evans, Reuben Brown, David Tranter, and David Grubin, my collaborator on *Language Matters. Ma Barang!* Now we've got it!

At the Wailing Wall *(p. 97)* Composed spontaneously then tucked into the Wall for "On the Road With Bob Holman," Yiddish/Ladino/Hebrew episode. Ram Devineni, producer/director. Beatriz Seigner, producer/cinematographer.

Clogwyni o Llyn/Cliffs of Llyn *(p. 97)* Written at Nant Gwrtheyrn, the magical Welsh language immersion program, with help from Graham Davies, in preparation for *Language Matters*.

Remnants Peformance (Life Liberty, Pursuit of Poetry) *(p. 98)* European tour for Mouth Almighty Records, 1997, with Maggie Estep, Wammo, and Mike Ladd.

Costa Rica Poems Papa (Alhaji Papa Susso) and I were invited to the International Poetry Festival of Costa Rica in San José in 2008. Beside doing our main show for the crowds at the capital, they sent the two of us off to Limón, in the indigenous people's territory, where we canoed all the way to Panama. These poems are what happened: **Poetry Reading in the Jungle** *(p. 99)* The poets: Gabriel Rosenstock, Miguel Barnet, Ahmad Al-Shahawi, Salah Ahsssan and **So Much Depends on a Red Wheelbarrow Glazed With Rainwater Beside the White Chickens** *(p. 101)* Frank Baez *is* the Marilyn Monroe of Santo Domingo, DR! I added a word to one of the poems in this section in honor of the present (shout out to Otto Barz, publisher/editor).

Poets of Medellín *(p. 104)* Written while at the International Poetry Festival in Medellín. Thanks to Fernando Rendón. This is the world's greatest poetry festival. 4,000 people attend the final reading. The great majority can't afford to buy a book. So they approach the poets with individual lines, written on scraps of paper to which poets affix signatures. Thanks to my Spanish translator, Sol Gaitán, who performed with me in Colombia.

Grandly and Centrally *(p. 106)* Commissioned for a reading at Grand Central Station on her Centenary. I just let it fly as I wrote, and, in performance, figure it out as I go. But this is no way to write poem! Quatrains first six stanzas, even seems to have a form when verses 1 and 3 have anaphora of title. Then in verse 4 Walt Whitman wanders in (Maddening(ly)), Meddlesome(ly), from his "City of Wharves"). Scattershot rhyme scheme: AAAA, BBCC, AAAA. Then in the 4th verse, internal rhymes kick in: D-D/A-A/E-E/F-F. 5th verse switches from internal rhymes to short lines: GGGF (assuming that "dish" and "quick" are slant rhymes!). Verse 6 switches to six lines for some reason: HHGGGG, and Verse 7 has five line: IIGGG. Line 8 through the end goes back to quatrains, with erratic rhymes: JJKK, LLML, NOPO (NOPO!), QRSR, TTTA, AAAU. Finally, in Verse 12, Frank O'Hara wanders in, from "The Day Lady Died."

All I know is that, when sung, it sounds like a poem.

Walking Brooklyn Bridge *(p. 108)* was written while walking Brooklyn Bridge. Thinking about Walt Whitman crossing Brooklyn ferry. Old Gray Beard seems to own this bridge. but he only saw it once. It was not here when he lived on Ryerson Street or anywhere else in Brooklyn or Manhattan. He went home to Trenton as it was constructed, returned once. Miss you, Walt. Published in Steve Cannon's *A Gathering of the Tribes* at the insistence of Ra.

Praise Poems

This section is dedicated to Papa Susso. Often, African oral poets have been simply termed "praise singers," but that is just one of many tasks in the oral poets' resume (see Thomas Hale's *Griots and Griottes*). Maybe the reason it's so often mentioned is because it makes up a large part of a griot's income. In general, a praise poem goes on as long as money is being danced to the poet. The poet sings the praise song, the people dance to the kora and poem. And then money appears. It's a poetic economy that includes money, which is one reason the oral tradition continues in Africa. The poet also earns djellasi at naming ceremonies and weddings. No music at funerals. That comes from New Orleans. But other parts of the griot's job—teaching, resolving real estate disputes, helping people with genealogy, handing out the dicta of the chiefs—are often unpaid. Many people in the U.S. become embarrassed when the praise poem starts to take flight. I hope the humor and hyperbole in these praise poems help mitigate and bring on the love to the Praised.

Papa Susso Christmas Praise Poem *(p. 111)* Alhaji Papa Susso has been my way into the life of the griot and the tradition of Praise Poetry, since the year 2000. We've travelled all over and performed many many times—the whole center section of *Sing This One Back To Me*, and the title too, comes from our collaborations and translations. I hear from him quite often during Ramadan. At Christmas/Hanukkah time he should hear from me, correct? I'm not nearly the good Muslim he is.

Praise Poem World Heavyweight Championship Bout 2000 *(p. 112* This poem opened up my challenge to Sherman Alexie and is the basis for several of the poems in this section. Because this is how history gets passed on, it's important in the oral tradition to name everybody, and I hope I got the whole Taos scene mentioned in this poem. Peter Rabbit was none too pleased that the poem came in over five minutes, thus triggering the Anne Waldman Rule, but Annie MacNaughton told me she was happy I went all out.

"Salmonfull" in line one is an attempt at acknowledgement of Sherman's Salish roots; rhymes with "Luminous Animal" (L.5) which is the name of Peter and Annie's band; "Nightbesotted" "Anti-school" (L.6) completes the rhyme and refers to the bouts being the historical precedent for the poetry slam ("Where the Audience reigns" [L.7]).

cf. **Performance Poem** *(p. 9)* was another poem performed at the Bout.

Poema de Alabanza para Pablo Neruda *(p. 117)* Commissioned by David Spellman. The Madonna and Julia Roberts references refer to the recording released with the movie, "The Postman."

On the Street Named Pedro Pietri *(p. 119)* Pedro and I met in the poetry trenches but when we became co-workers at the CCF CETA Artists Project we began to co-produce events ranging from The Big Mouth Poets giant group poetry readings to The Double Talk Show—the world's only late night TV Talk Show *not* on TV. The first time I ever raised money for a poetry project was for for Pedro and Diane Burns to fly to Managua in 1988 for the "U.S. Poets Invade Nicaragua Tour" which resulted in the two of them getting married there, setting off an international poetry incident. Pedro is in *Poetry Spots* and *The United States of Poetry*. This poem was written for the street-sign-unveiling of Rev. Pedro Pietri Way, on 3rd Street between avenues B and C, in NYC in 2006.

Nia! Imani! Kuja Jakaleah! *(p. 120)* are the first words on the first cut of Sekou's epic "The Blue Oneness of Dreams" (Mouth Almighty/Mercury). Like any good griot, Sekou opens his "book" (he never published a book; well, Robert Feaster published a chapbook, but that's another story) he was too busy putting out records, fronting bands, creating record labels (with Bill Adler, my founding partner and who named the label "Mouth Almighty") with a shout out to the Universal Ear. I remember Baraka crying at Sekou's memorial. I remember the kidney dialysis paraphernalia delivered to his motel room on the "Life, Liberty and Pursuit of Poetry" U.S. tour with Maggie Estep and The Last Poets. I remember his improv trio, "Everlasting Life," with Gylan Kain and Kurt Lamkin.

Tato's Hat *(p. 122)* Tato Laviera, proving once and for all that *la carreta* did make a u-turn.

Lester Afflick *(p. 123)* was a proud poet member of the original Gathering of the Tribes living room. *I Dream About You Baby,* his posthumous collection, his only.

Hell and High Water Steve Cannon Praise Poem *(p. 124)* What can I say about Steve? A footnote to Steve means putting your foot in your mouth, I could say that. We go back so far we ain't ever coming back. He taught me everything I know. More love for the Blind Guy. His poems are the oral tradition, the oral tradition is his life and vice versa and verso vice. This one appears in "Tribes 15," which is so controversial it probably never existed.

Bang *(p. 125)* Jazz violinist Billy Bang and I had a band that performed numerous times (2002-2005) as Bang Holman, usually a trio, sometimes a quartet. Tod Nicholson usually played bass, Tyshawn Shorey was most often drums. We performed "Jazzes," "Ornettes," and "Black Herman," which was based on a story Billy told me. The music was great, the blend was what it's all about, and there has never been more fun art. Miss you, Billy.

If I Were To Throw My Money *(p. 128)* *Flying Words*, Peter Cook and Kenny Lerner, introduced me to American Sign Language poetry at Joe Flaherty's Bridge Festival for Writers and Books in Rochester, NY, in the early '80s. I've produced three or four of their video poems since then. It's the irony of ironies: American Sign Language, any sign language, cannot be written down. In that way it's the essence of Oral Tradition. The essence of the oral tradition is lived by those who cannot speak. ASL is also an endangered language. And like all endangered languages, it has its own particular back story. In this case, it's science that is the root of the language decline. Cochlear implant– what parent should face the question of mainstreaming your child with no guarantee of how successful the operation will be? Or, on the other hand, standing strong for your community?

The words in **Praise Poem James Siena** *(p. 130)* are taken from interviews with James, formed into a concrete poem along the contours of one of his paintings. See the results in *A Couple of Ways of Doing Something* alongside Chuck Close's portrait of James.

Praise Alex Katz *(p. 135)* Commissioned by Rob Storr for an event honoring Alex.

The Melting Point of Ice: Jean–Michel Basquiat *(p. 136)* was comissioned for an event at the Whitney Museum.

Claire Poem *(p. 139)* Happy Belated Birthday to Claire Danes, whose first poem I read when she was five years old. It was about a snowman.

2 Peter Rabbit *(p. 140)* Obit orbit Praise for poet and co-founder of World Heavyweight Championship Poetry Bout. King of Taos.

Turning 50 At The Circus *(p. 141)* Anne and Peter were divorced and remarried so many times that at his death they couldn't remember which state they were in. Anne: radical poet and Pueblo language activist—her high school students at the Taos Public Day School were the first-ever to get a varsity letter in Poetry.

Patricia Spears Jones Praise Poem *(p. 142)* Circa 1978 Patricia, Sara Jones, Fay Chiang and Sandra Maria Estevez joined forces to edit *Ordinary Women*, world's first multi-cultural all-women anthology. As far as we were concerned it was the Neighborhood. Adrienne Rich wrote the introduction. I was honored to participate in the 25th reunion.

Jessica Hagedorn Massive Praise Poem *(p. 143)* Commissioned by the Asian American Writers Workshop. Dearest friend, our kids went to Pompeii Daycare together—the parents co-op, not the volcanic ruins. It was there that Jessica came up with the idea that I should wear a Santa Claus suit for the holiday do. Her Gangster Choir was the original model for a slammin' po band and her novels define "poet's novel."

One Letter Poem *(p. 147)* Progenitor of *Schule für Dichtung* in Vienna, Ida Hintze created a poetry all his own. The session I taught in Vienna in 2010 involved a living collaboration, 24-hour, nonstop creation of a breathing poem. He turned his body into an alphabet, or was it the other way round?

Salmon Blues *(p. 149)* Bob Carroll, queer performance artist who crashed at everybody's house in the early 80's, was the model of political activist performer hippie Angel of Light. He introduced me to Michael McClure in a San Francisco living room performance and together we populated a Lower East Side living poetry performance life. His *Salmon Show*, performed balanced on one leg with a six pack in one hand until all beers were distributed, imagined the U.S. Economy as the Life Cycle of a Salmon. When he was blind and dying of AIDS, he asked me if I could go for a walk with him in the woods and just leave him there. I thought we could do everything, but that I could not do.

(Words for) Lord Buckley *(p. 150)* is a poet IMHO. I was proud to get "The Train" into *The United States of Poetry*.

Epithalamium *(p. 151)* Oh how I wanted to be "Maria the Korean Bride's" 50th husband, to marry her in Times Square! I bought ten raffle tickets, thinking that should tilt the odds. My pal Ram bought a single ticket and you can guess what happened. Nevertheless the happy couple asked me to be Best Man on that wonderful occasion, presided over by the head of the Rents Too Damn High Party—cake by The Cake Master.

The Interference of Time on Love *(p. 152)* Dear friends, Jan Hashey and Yasuo Minigawa were the ideal couple and best friends of Elizabeth and mine. They decided to get married after living together thirty years. No way you don't get a poem for that.

A Nice Little Chat *(p. 153)* Suzanne Bocanegra and David Lang met when Elizabeth and I and the girls were at the American Academy in Rome and we were happy to see their love sprout into three children, all of whom got bar- or bat-mitzvahed with Praise Poems. Judah is the youngest.

Praise Bonnet *(p. 157)* A sonnet for Sam Abrams, cranky pothead radical, one of the originals at the St. Marks Poetry Project. Sam was a professor at Rochester when the Nuyorican Poet's Cafe was revived in 1989 and became one of our strongest supporters. We'd all camp out at his and Barbara's house in Rochester and go to Nick Tahou's for a garbage plate (french fries, cheese, mayo, franks, lunchmeats and various other stuff, all mixed together—Rochester's national dish) at midnight.

J'Praise *(p. 158)* Jerry Rothenberg is my mentor. Allen Ginsberg once told me, "He saved us all twenty years." His *Technicians of the Sacred* and *Shaking the Pumpkin* are ur texts for oral tradition/endangered language poetry. Fifty years after *TOTS* was published, a poem of Papa Susso's and mine was included in the second edition. Time is a donut—dunk it.

David Amram *(p. 159)* invented the Jazz Poetry Reading with Jack Kerouac. David is always on and always in the middle of whatever it is. Whenever he spends the night at my house there is no night, next thing you know it's morning.

For Jack Micheline *(p. 160)* When Jack heard me perform "Rock'n'Roll Mythology" at Intersection in North Beach, he told me it was the first new poem he'd heard since the Beats. He himself was a true Beat.

Praise Ed Sanders *(p. 160)* The Fugs in 1967 showed me there was life in poetry. Ed and Tuli showed the way and I've been on it ever since. Hello to Miriam. This poem was written for a mega-birthday rumpus in 1997 at Woodstock, a few years before a production of Ed's play, *The Rebel Café*, which I directed, opened at the Bowery Poetry Club.

My Man Lev *(p. 165)* Where did these 8 1/2 x 11 mimeo posters around the Columbia campus come from? It was 1969 and there was going to be an open mic poetry reading at Forlini's Third Phase. Knowing there would be a huge crowd, I showed up early, 7:45. At five after 8 the first poet showed up—Don Lev. I had met the Minnesota labor poet Thomas McGrath on board a student ship to Europe the year before my first poet sighting. I was studying with Kenneth Koch at Columbia— my Walt Whitman. But Don Lev was the first working/street poet I came in contact with. He took me under his sweet wing, eventually giving me my first reading. He's The Poet in *Putney Swope*, reading "Hyn, my word, Hyn," to Putney and Fidel Castro on a Harlem street corner. I still don't understand why there were only two other students who showed up that day at Forlini's. The eternally open mic is the essence of democracy.

A Little Something *(p. 166)* Oh what a wonderful poet, Enid Dame! This poem written for a festschrift upon her death. Enid and Don Lev, a single heart, now buried together in New Montefiore Cemetery in Queens.

Growing up in Cincinnati, **Frank Robinson** *(p. 167)* was my favorite Red. David Kirschenbaum commissioned this one for *Boog City*.

Hanlon Stuart *(p. 168)* Friendship is indeed underrated. Stu and I met on the first day of orientation at Columbia and BFF. He's the lawyer, I'm the poet. This poem supposedly got him in a lot of hot water because of Geronimo Pratt and the SLA. Our kids grew up together, our wives both died. He knows where the pills are.

Ode to the Lemon Ice King *(p. 172)* Commissioned by City Lore. Steve Zeitlin, co-author.

The Prairie *(p. 175)* Jim Gandolfini read at the Bowery Poetry Club's benefit, Hollywood Does Poetry. I suggested (gently) he read Emily Dickinson but he stuck with Bukowski. A few days before the reading I got a phone call: "Bob, it's Jim Gandolfini. I don't know if you know this, but I have a little business, a laundromat, out in LA, and there's a flood. I don't think I can make it to the Benefit." "Jim," I said, "This is for poetry. People bought tickets so they could hear *you* read. Rethink this." Pause. "Ok. I'll be there." So now I tell people, I twisted Tony Soprano's arm. He prepared for the reading at the Mars Bar. Read beautifully from the heart. He was all heart.

Bird With No Mouth *(p. 175)* I'd see Philip Seymour Hoffman in the neighborhood. Brilliant and just one of us.

Last Line *(p. 179)* Founder of LaMama, Ellen Stewart was everybody's mother. The Poetry Project-La Mama Poets Theater Festivals were the ultimate poetry-theater collaborations. Quirk: she never would allow the color green on stage.

Sowing Stars *(p. 180)* Helen Tworkov, founder of *Tricycle* magazine, good friend of Elizabeth's, good friend of mine. This one first read in her cabin on Cape Breton.

All Praise Cecil Taylor *(p. 181)* first appeared in Quincy Troupe's NYU literary magazine, "Black Renaissance Noir," and later was selected for *Best American Poetry 2019*, edited by Major Jackson and David Lehman (Scribner's). Quincy also published *A True Account of Ntozake Shange's* . . . in "BRN."

All Together, Call Together *(p. 181)* Annually and then biennially, the *People's Poetry Gathering,* a collaboration first between Poet's House and City Lore, later between City Lore and Bowery, was the model of orality and literacy in congress. This poem was commissioned as the prolegomenon of the documentary about the Gathering. All thanks to Steve Zeitlin and also to the mighty staffs of the organizations, who eventually threw down and said, "It's just too damn much work." PPG, 1997–2002, RIP. [This version found its way into the United States Department of Arts and Culture (not a government agency) People's State of the Union, under guidance of Arlene Goldbard and Adam Horowitz.]

This Is It! *(p. 184)* was published in *Word: An Anthology* (*Gathering of the Tribes*, Steve Cannon).

CPSIA information can be obtained
at www.ICGtesting.com
Printed in the USA
FSHW010048251019
63367FS